ECONOMIE

Patterns of hea

BILL SHARPE

Many of the insights from these essays have been put into practice at Watershed, Bristol. A publication about the process, 'Producing the Future: Understanding Watershed's Role in Ecosystems of Cultural Innovation' by Graham Leicester & Bill Sharpe, is available from Watershed. For further information, and to register to receive a copy, please go to www.watershed.co.uk/reports

Contents

Can we use ecological thinking to understand how the arts work in society? That is the disarmingly simple question from which this set of essays arose. The role of creativity is increasingly acknowledged for its economic importance and contribution to all aspects of our life. But at the same time those who work in what is generally described as the cultural sector struggle to explain what they are doing in its own terms, without having to justify it by other measures and outcomes.

In the International Futures Forum[1] we have been working on this issue for several years with a wide variety of partners. At the centre of the issue we have found that everyone is struggling to talk about 'value'. It is no good trying to relate all the value of the arts and culture to monetary valuations, and equally unhelpful to try and justify the arts as some sort of special interest cut off from all our other priorities. The arts seem to suffer a severe form of the same problems that afflict our attempts to resolve conflicts between the health of the environment and economic growth – just how can we talk about things that matter without immediately having to put a price on them?

We believe we have come up with some fresh concepts and language to tackle this dilemma. We find the problem lies precisely in the default assumption that there is only one economy in our lives – 'the' economy which is the one based on money.

Our position is that there are *many* economies, of which the one based on money is just one, and that they all contribute to the health and sustainability of our shared lives; each one supports a pattern that combines individual and shared valuation in a unique way. Our habit of taking 'economic value' to mean 'monetary value' is at best misleading, and in general nonsensical – most value has nothing whatever to do with money. No one economy should be elevated into the sole determinant of value: they must all be kept individually healthy, with currents of value passing between them in mutually sustainable ways.

The essence of ecological thinking is to see the pattern of life as a connected whole. There is just one overall ecosystem of our lives, and within it there are many economies that support different ways of sharing and exchanging things, knowledge, and experience.

The monetary economy is all about alienable value – it rests on the idea of moving around 'property' – things we own and can give to other people. We have no simple way of describing the opposite – things that we own but cannot give to other people. What things mean to me in my own life is inalienable – I can share my taste in music but I cannot give it to you. It is proper to me, a quality of my life. So, making meaning for ourselves stands at the other economic pole of our lives; the economy of meaning is the economy of inalienable value. We find we can discuss art as the currency of this economy; art is the currency of experience, putting our unique individual experiences into motion amongst us as shared meaning.

This approach has several benefits. As soon as the money economy is de-throned from its position as the arbiter of all 'economic' value, we can start to bring ecological concepts into the heart of economic thinking, understanding economies as patterns of shared life. We can explore what keeps each economy healthy, what sort of wealth each one accumulates, what sort of policies are most supportive of innovation and sustainability and so on. We can also explore boundaries, and how resources should move between economies in ways that are mutually sustainable and do not corrupt them. We can make distinctions between 'outcomes' that are intrinsic to an economy and its proper functioning, and those that entail using its resources for other purposes in other economies.

We are finding this new way of thinking breaks free from the eternal cycle of arguments about intrinsic value, instrumentalism and so on and speaks to the reality of the world of producers who are constantly reconciling meaning and money as an active creative process itself. It also brings into the foreground the role everyone in society plays as co-producers of every sort of value, and helps us focus on enhancing the artistic potential of every individual in our shared cultural life.

This work is structured as a set of essays. It is in the nature of an essay to be a place to put forward opinions, and try out ideas. The concepts and language here are novel. We are keen to build a wider conversation to find out if they stand up to robust critique and are useful for both policy makers and those who practise the arts in all spheres of life and need to explain what it is they do. There is a companion document, a case study of the Watershed Media Centre in Bristol, which develops the practical implications of the ideas in more detail[2]. These essays develop the core concepts and give the background sources. The two documents share much material.

The **first essay** sets the scene by opening up the basic contrast between ecological and economic ways of talking, and points towards how to relate them through the way we make meaning in our lives.

The **second essay** shows how the concept of value arises naturally from discussions of pattern and identity. The foundation is to see individual lives as always going forward in dynamic patterns of relationship, and to regard value as a perspective on the pattern from the point of view of a life within it.

In the **third essay** I put forward the central ideas of this investigation: we can generalise the idea of an economy beyond that of the pattern created by money, and this general concept of economy allows us to move in a principled way between the third person languages of ecology and economics that *describe* our lives, and the first person language of experience that concerns what it is like to *live* a life. These ideas come together in the proposition that titles the essay: *art is the currency of experience.*

The remaining two essays are a working out in more detail of the main ideas.

The **fourth essay** concerns how we can think about the way all the different economic patterns of our lives work together, and what is necessary for them to be both individually and collectively healthy.

The **final essay** is a change of gear. It reports on the findings from our first experiment in applying these ideas in a practical context. The practical and theoretical work went along in parallel, so this is all very preliminary, but it gives a flavour of the way that we see these ideas working out in policy and in practice.

Prelude

Try the following experiment, at least in your mind's eye. Take some money in your hand and go out into the garden (I hope you have one, or at least somewhere you keep a few tubs of flowers). Now try and give the money to the flowers to help them grow. Or perhaps you can bury it and it will nourish them; or, … this is plainly futile. Pick some of the flowers and bring them in. Arrange them in a vase and put them on the table to make it look attractive and invite a close friend round for dinner. Discuss a favourite book, film, or whatever, and have a good conversation. What made the conversation flow? Was it the dinner or was it the history and current content of shared experience? Where did your ideas, and your friend's, come from? Now take the flowers back to the compost heap – that will help the garden – and remember to tell so-and-so about that new idea you just had while talking to your friend.

Homo Ecologicus and Homo Economicus

> *Ecology: the science of the economy of animals and plants.*
> Oxford English Dictionary

ECOLOGICAL thinking sees the properties and behaviours of parts as determined by the pattern of the whole. Rather than look at an individual species, we look at the interactions of all the organisms, and how they are maintained by, and themselves maintain, the overall flows of resources. Thus the trees on a mountainside themselves play a part in the formation of the clouds and rainfall that maintain them and that contribute to the viability of other species around them. Lose the trees and the cycle of rain is lost, the heat of the sun dries the ground, and the whole ecosystem moves to a much lower level of fecundity.

Economic thinking is particularly concerned with issues of resources and how they are allocated. Consideration of such issues lies naturally within an ecological framework. However, in our common parlance, 'the economy' has come to refer to the pattern of activity that is supported by our use of money, and we generally have money in mind when we refer to 'economic value'. From this habit of language and thought much confusion arises that this set of essays is trying to clear up. We will be developing the idea of an economy in later essays, but for now, in order to introduce the discussion, we'll stay with the conventional sense of 'an economy' to mean what goes on when we take things to market and trade them for money.

In the case of natural resources it is very clear that the ecosystem 'works' without the need for any money to circulate; it is the input of energy from the sun, and the flow of resources such as water through rainfall, and other material exchanges that sustain it. When an ecosystem interacts with the economy then an additional dynamic is set up. If you want to log a forest for timber sustainably then you must understand the ecosystem that maintains its viability, or you will be in danger of taking too much from it, and tipping it into decline.

What is this economic dynamic – what happens when an ecosystem becomes entwined with economic activity? At the simplest level, some components of the ecosystem become detached from their role in the system, in which they and the system maintain each other through their mutual and original properties, and get put to some 'other' use which bears no systemic relationship to the health or viability of the original system.

I cut down a tree and take it away to make furniture. Two things happened here: the tree came down, and it was removed. The first would happen naturally at some point, but its removal inevitably changes the ecosystem. The pattern of resource circulation that was a part of the system that produced the tree has been disturbed. The cutting down might also matter because the seeds might not yet have been produced; or they might need fire to germinate, and felling may change the undergrowth such that the conditions for fire and germination are lost, etc.

The basic point is that ecosystems do not exist 'for' any purpose – they just are what they are, and they develop along certain paths based on the conditions they are in. Once we start to connect them with economies, in which parts of them are 'for something' that lies outside the ecosystem, then we perturb them, and thereby we become instrumental in their continued viability. We create a mutual dependence between our own needs and the needs of the ecosystem. If we need it for something, to make furniture or whatever, then it also needs us to ensure that our perturbations don't destroy its essential system properties. At the most basic level our responsibility is to ensure we do not draw down too much resource at once, and that we allow the system time to 'recover'; in other words, we rely on some self-maintaining, homeostatic process to put back the things we are removing, or remove the things we are dumping.

A more sophisticated understanding of the mutual relationship between an economy and the ecosystems on which it depends would be to start to think of the economic activity as an integral component of the larger ecosystem, so that the cycles of activity all become mutually sustaining. This is the way of some (not all) traditional cultures of sustainable agriculture, in which resources are returned to the soil in closed cycles. It is a way, too, that is in the vanguard of thinking about the economic sustainability of modern economies under the general notion of 'industrial ecology' which seeks to see all economic activity through the pattern of mutually self-maintaining systems, just like natural ecosystems, and in balance with those natural ecosystems on which they depend.

What ecological and economic approaches share is that they look at our lives as coordinated patterns of activity. Coordination is a useful concept because it allows us to see how patterns arise amongst activities that may be any mixture of collaborative and competitive – the lives of predators and prey are coordinated but competitive, while bees and flowers are coordinated and collaborative. The core of what we have to do is to bring this approach to bear on the entire pattern of our lives, without first splitting it up into a part that we call 'ecological' and another part that we call 'economic'. We only live one life, but we take part in many patterns. How are all these patterns coordinated? How might we view every pattern both ecologically and economically?

To get a sense of this approach let's start with a book reading circle – a simple component of a healthy ecosystem in which literature circulates. People have got together to discuss the draft of a new book by one of the members. The book itself is the result of a 'making' – the sustained use of the imagination on the part of the author to bring forth a world. Each word put in its place brings meanings and echoes of meanings together from the entire cultural context, both private to the author and shared with the surrounding society. As the book is read and commented on, meaning is made in the room, with each participant bringing their unique response to the book into the conversation, bringing shades of meaning into play. Everyone who joins the conversation changes the conversation. Each utterance is itself a fleeting 'making' – it brings together strands of meaning and weaves them into the emerging shared pattern in the room. Perhaps one relates the book to a personal anecdote, another hears similarities with the technique of another writer, and a third explores what appears to be a psychological inconsistency in the plot, and so on.

As meaning is made, transformed, woven, the cultural world of each person is further enriched. The next conversation in this or another book circle will be different because of this encounter. The author will have become aware of new ripples of meaning, previously unimagined.

Perhaps one of the members is a teacher and goes back to the classroom with a refreshed understanding and a new approach to the works to be taught. Another finds the story quite haunting, throwing a fresh light on life, and mentions it to a friend facing a challenge in their life. And so the ripples spread, reflect, interfere, add and cancel, reverberating through the cultural ecosystem of meaning.

We can view this activity through the lens of both ecological and economic language.

Why is it helpful to view this as an ecosystem? Because, in the account we have just given, the meaning both enriches and is enriched by the encounters of all the actors in the system; it circulates amongst them. It is traded in its own terms rather than translated into any proxy. There are several ways to see this.

First, the only way to enhance the conversation was for each member to engage with it as deeply as possible, bringing to it their own capacity to build on and enrich the meaning in the room. The only inputs of importance were their own experience, their own webs of significance and the connections they could make between them and the conversation. Just as you cannot make the flower grow by giving it money – you must give it air, light, water – so you cannot make the conversation grow by giving it anything except the meaning from which it is formed.

Second, although there were 'outcomes' in the lives of the people who took part, these were incidental and unplanned to the event itself. No-one could be responsible for these outcomes except the people who created them post facto. This is just like saying that as a flower grows in the garden it is constantly interacting with all the other plants and insects around it, and with the weather, and each interaction plays its part in creating the conditions of growth for this particular plant in this particular place – growth, however, which only it can do.

Third, any attempt to turn the meaning into being 'for' something will, like taking a tree for wood from a forest, change the basis of the ecosystem. Suppose the author takes the comments and quotes them on their website to promote the book. Or go further, and suppose that the friends were invited round and given a meal to discuss the book just for this purpose. Then there is no reason to suppose they will not have a good and stimulating conversation. However, by connecting the conversation to this extrinsic goal there is a breaking of systemic connections. It is likely that just like taking a tree from a forest, the reading circle can regenerate, but if time after time the circle is used purely as a marketing meeting to harvest promotional quotes, then it will probably degrade and lose its vitality. This process is simply the result of connecting the functioning of an ecosystem to another process that deflects some of the essential circulation of energy and resources for a different purpose.

Looking back at this ecological description we can equally read it as an economic one.

First, there was an activity of sharing and exchanging going on, in that each person brought their own experience to bear, and took away new understandings for themselves. Second, the outcomes in their lives represented the transition from a shared process of the conversation to some sort of 'use' value, just as happens when we bring something home from the market. And finally, we do of course move our cultural outputs to and fro between embedding them in the act of making artistic meaning, and promoting them as economic products, and we have found ways to do this that mostly work quite well for us. The issue really is one of ensuring that the relationship between different uses does not damage the integrity of the systems.

Homo Poeticus – making the patterns of our lives

We learn words by rote, but not their meaning; that must be paid for with our life-blood, and printed in the subtle fibres of our nerves.

Latimer, in *The Lifted Veil*, George Eliot

IMAGINE, you enter a room where a conversation is going on. The boundary of the conversation has now shifted, bringing you from outside to inside. Even if you say nothing you have already changed the conversation by being within it. You have changed the significance of what is said, because your own lived experience now interacts with those present to shade the meaning of every word: an innocent joke may now be too near the bone, an opinion may become a judgement, or a serious intent may now seem merely a playful possibility. The integrity of the conversation now has you as a living participant in its creation. Something different will come of it.

Two living systems cannot interact without consequence. Their fields of meaning connect, and each now finds itself laying down a new path in the walking[3]: will our paths merge, cross, diverge; is that for good or for ill, and who shall say?

Where does the meaning in a conversation come from? What has been traded? Words pass between us, but meaning does not travel from one person to another, like a piece of traded goods in exchange for money; it is made in the moment, borrowing from the lived history of everyone in the room, and it lives on in the new patterns of significance that each person takes away.

We encounter the world through our senses from a particular point of view. We find ourselves within a particular horizon, in a particular place. No matter how hard we try, we cannot see anything from all sides at once. All our sense of the world arises from this embodied, active, self-centred relationship to the world; our awareness of the world and of ourselves arise together, each mutually determining the other.

We communicate about experience in two sorts of language. Turning away from our selves, exploring the physical world, we use our reason to bring order and comprehension to our perceptions, removing our particular, contingent point of view. Although the sun appears to go around the earth, and some of the stars appear to wander erratically through the sky, we find that we can restore consistency by de-centring our perceptions and conceiving of a sun-centred solar system. In such efforts we aim to remove from our conceptions the significance of the world for our own particular selves. What is true is what is true for all people at all times. This is the scientific project. How far we might bring this way of thinking back to the heart of ourselves we do not yet know. This is the language of science spoken by Homo Ecologicus and Homo Economicus.

Turning towards our selves as living, contingent beings, we find life proceeds through many individuals, and each person is both an instance of the old and a birth of the new, enacting new possibilities of life. My particular point of view is of ultimate relevance to me, where I am now: shall I take this path or that, love this person, die for this idea? In each choice I enact meaning in the world for this particular, peculiar contingent self that I am. I explore the possibilities for my life, and in so doing I change not only my path, but the path of the world for all, because I am part of the world. What is true is what is true for me, but also for you, for us, for us all, and is always in motion, never finally resolved.

This is the language of Homo Poeticus – the maker of meaning. It concerns the perpetual dilemma dance of every life between the demands of being for itself and being as part of the whole within which all life goes forward. We share life, but must each live our own. We are part of the pattern, but must determine the possibilities of that pattern for our own self.

There is no shortcut to finding the meaning of love, pain, happiness, or any other inalienable quality of our lives. They cannot be traded, but they can be brought into shared stories that we tell each other, and that make us what we are. This language must always be in motion, linking one life to another, so that its meaning can be constantly remade through the encounter of each life with the possibilities in front of it, both for itself, and for the whole.

We have banks that coin the currency of trade in those things we can pass among us. We have art that coins meaning that we can share only by living it, bringing it alongside the choices that we must make of which song to sing, which story to join. How can we speak both languages with integrity? That is the subject of the remaining essays.

2: Patterns of Shared Life

Meaningful patterns, but never abiding ones.
Charles Sherrington[4]

The start of our inquiry into value is to understand how individual lives are formed and lived in dynamic patterns of relationship.

A pattern comes about when things which have some degrees of freedom are related to each other such that for a while their behaviour is coordinated: drops of moisture in a cloud, living organisms in an ecosystem, couples in a dance, children in a family, citizens in a nation, and so on. Life is lived amongst many such patterns which relate one life to others and to their surroundings.

We will see that the concept of value arises naturally from discussions of pattern and identity: exploring just how patterns of the whole bear upon the ongoing identity and viability of a life within it. A particular living identity is the origin of a perspective on the rest of the world in which it lives; this perspective is the field of value for that life in the pattern of relationships in which it is living.

Running through this discussion will be the steadfast refusal to adopt any particular origin from which all other patterns can be understood. Only if we see all patterns as co-determined and constantly in motion will we be able to achieve the integration we seek between our understanding of the world and what it feels like to live in it, between the patterns that we all share and the particular life that each of us must live.

Emergent patterns

Actual time is a constant. Your time is perception. Swing time is a collective action. Everyone in jazz is trying to create a more flexible alternative to actual time... You're in time when your actions are perceptive and flexible enough to flow inside that ultimate constant – swing.

Wynton Marsalis[5]

THERE is a fascinating little experiment you can do with a couple of spoons and three pieces of string. Hang each of the spoons from a piece of string that is tied like a washing line between two chairs. Set the first spoon swinging while the other hangs still. As the first spoon swings, little by little the second one starts to swing also, but not in time with the first, picking up more and more energy until it is the one swinging and the first one comes almost to rest. Then the process reverses, and the first one picks up again while the second one comes to rest. And so on, and on. Add more spoons and the patterns become even more varied and fascinating.

Each spoon produces a behaviour that is quite different from what it would produce on its own, and the cause cannot be found in anything less than the complete configuration of spoons and string. This is a simple demonstration of dynamic coordination, in which things link together to create emergent patterns that change what each of the participants can do. If we zoom in and look at one spoon hanging there and try to understand its behaviour without seeing the other one and how they are coupled, we will never work out what is going on. Worse, we may try to find a source of the mysterious rhythm of its behaviour in the inner world of the spoon as it senses the world at each moment, and then acts out its ebbing and flowing cycle of behaviour for its own purposes. Or we may locate the origin of this behaviour in some pervading rhythmic force. We would never make those mistakes, would we?

By the same token, where does a story come from? Does it belong to the teller, the listeners, the society, the culture, or is it some sort of entity that propagates itself? Surely, we can only understand it as part of a pattern of coordination amongst all the lives that pass it on; a pattern that is a property of the whole, in which everything participates, but which nothing less than the whole originates. This is true both of a folk story that lives only in the constant retelling, or a great work of literature, that arises in a moment of time and then shapes the culture that follows it.

Pick up a pencil and start to write some notes about these essays on a pad of paper. Where is the boundary between you and the world? Is it between your hand and the pencil, between the pencil and paper, between you and words you write, or perhaps around you, your thoughts and the papers... Our sense of the boundary is built by our experience with the tools that we use. People with leprosy who have lost the sense of touch in their fingers but can still move them can be given a glove with touch sensors that are relayed to a sensitive part of their skin such as the forehead. After a while using the gloves, a remarkable remapping of the sensations takes place, such that they have the sensation of 'feeling' with their hands. In a similar way, as we start to use an unfamiliar word, or sing a new song, it ties us into a pattern of thoughts that move from being other to being our own, part of our own experience, but linked to the other.

The vortex in a stream, the words written on our notepad, our experience of being in the world, are momentary patterns which must be understood as qualities of the constant to and fro between part and whole. We must see that from new connections, new qualities arise. The qualities of life are renewed, or brought into being for the first time, by the way that relationships are configured. Our senses can be renewed, and our sense of the world reformed, by the things that link our lives. Artefacts and arts are things made; the pencil and the poem are made, used, and elaborated with a skill passed down through generations to find new forms, shared in new ways on the digital devices in our pockets. When we ask what something is for, then our starting point must always be to understand the role it plays in configuring patterns between parts and the whole, since it is only in these patterns that value for any part can arise at all.

Growth flows from relationship

> *Ubuntu Umutu ngumunta ngabantu*
> *A person is a person through other people.*
> African proverb

> *There cannot be social life without persons, but, equally, there can be no persons without social life.*
> Tim Ingold[6]

GROWTH flows from relationship. Look at a seed. It has a little store of energetic value, which it spends. First it must put down a tiny root, which starts the essential flow of water and nutrients. Then it can put up a shoot and start capturing the energy of the sun. Then as it builds its relationships with the world the internal processes of growth can get underway.

Look at a newborn lamb. At the moment of birth it finds itself in a nurturing relationship, in which the first lick from the mother, the first suck of milk, start the unfolding growth in the world of living relationships beyond the womb. Look at a human child. Beyond the processes of organic life, it must from the moment of birth also start the processes of human relationship, in which it will begin to discover the meaning of being a person. Touch, rhythm, smile, response, song. In each type of relationship a different internal potential is given direction and structure and is brought forth as a quality of shared life. And of course it flows in both directions: the mother is growing as a mother, as the baby is growing as a child.

It has been said that a baby that is not touched and held will die even if it has enough food and water to sustain life; the processes of growth arc through the fabric of human relationship[7]. This is most obviously true of all those forms of relationship that we think of as human 'culture' – those forms of shared life that are sustained through the generations by our active participation in them, of which language, music, tool-making are all defining examples. It has been observed that there is not enough information in a seed or embryo to describe the future form of the creature; the order emerges through the potential of the life growing within the appropriate pattern of relationship. This is true of organic life, and even more true of human culture; without a community of language there can be no language and no speakers.

Growth is both an unfolding of potential, and progressive transformation – change of form. Transformation is change in our internal patterns to create capabilities in the whole field of our relationships. We see this most dramatically in cases like the butterfly, where the lifecycle involves taking

the resources from one stage of development and completely re-ordering them into a new physical layout with new capabilities like flight. Most growth is not so obviously a visible change of form, but we increasingly understand that in the embodied structures of our mind equally fundamental changes take place as we grow. If these transformations do not take place when they should we may be damaged for life; much of our later potential is established in our early life.

So, a particular life is the trace of one pattern amongst the whole, in which structure supports relationship which in turn configures the processes of growth and change of structure.

Dynamic identity: the system in question

To see a World in a Grain of Sand
And a Heaven in a Wild Flower,
Hold Infinity in the palm of your hand
And Eternity in an hour.
William Blake[8]

THE things we see around us are all outcomes of the
processes of change. When we look at a mountain we
are seeing a snapshot of the result of the earth's dynamic
processes over billions of years; when we watch a bee
on a flower we are seeing part of the current state of the
unfolding of life on this particular planet; when we read a
story we are joining the human cultural journey. Each of our
human disciplines will reveal some particular aspect of these
processes: the physicists explore fundamental particles and
trace them back to the unimaginable big bang; evolutionary
theorists focus on our genes and the way that the algorithm
of evolution produces the bewildering variety of species;
and cultural historians follow the twists and turns of our
exploration of ourselves. And in this last exploration we turn
back into the centre of that complexity. We ourselves are
one particular nexus of all the processes of change that are
at play in the universe. To understand ourselves completely
would be to understand each of those processes in all its
fullness.

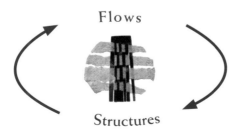

Flows

Structures

Fig 1: Living things are constantly remaking themselves

When we observe a pattern that involves dynamic behaviour we commonly call it a 'system', and we are recognising something that is actively maintaining an identity in the world. It has a certain structure which allows it to maintain flows of resources in and out of its context, and to engage with other systems. The flows support the structures which configure the flows, in a self-maintaining cycle. Thus, a tree grows by putting out leaves, and putting down roots, that capture the energy and nutrients that support the processes of growth that produce more leaves and roots. We can see this at the level of a cell, an organism, a tree, a person, or in the organisations of our human society from the family to the institutions of world governance. As long as the integrity of the structure is maintained it can keep going, but if it is damaged then its living processes may fail and it will disintegrate. Or the processes can be interrupted, and then again the system will be unable to maintain itself.

A dynamic pattern, or system, is a set of mutually supporting structures and processes that become visible at a certain choice of timescale and structural scale. Thus, the weather forecast in the evening shows the structure of fronts that will determine the weather processes (rain, wind, etc.) that are likely tomorrow. The pattern of fronts is itself a variable that changes with the seasons, and the seasonal processes are being changed by global warming, and in a few billion years the earth will evaporate like dew in the sunshine in an expanding sun, and the sun itself will return its elements to the cosmic processes which themselves move from big bang to big crunch as part of the multiverse in which particles and energy constantly interweave. Only after having chosen a particular timescale can we get to work understanding the intricacies of the particular processes at play, and how the structures configure them. For example, we might view a habitat that creates the right conditions for particular species, or the boundary of a cell that permits the

interior metabolic processes to
continue that themselves
maintain the boundary, or
human processes of cultivation
and social life all working
together in some intricate web
of mutual support.

Several things now become
clear. First, and most
fundamental, the identification
of what we will refer to as a
'system in question' (one that
we have chosen to study) is
just a matter of scale and does
not – in the nature of things cannot – define
anything of any permanence in the universal scale of things.
All structures enable processes that lead to new structures
that change the processes. Patterns come and go. Whether
we are a third person observer of a system of interest, or a
first person experiencer of a system in which we participate,
our designation of it *as* a system comprising certain identities
cannot help but be a particular, limited, point of view. There
is always a more encompassing scale than the one we have
chosen. To have a point of view on the world at all is to
view it as less than it is in its totality. Our science and our
experience are incomplete. An identity (a structure) appears
only as the relationship of a set of processes viewed from a
particular timescale.

Second, the identification of systems and the identities
we find within them is not arbitrary. Our point of view is
always incomplete, and we see things relatively, but *there is
something to see*. There is this mountain and not that plain;
the weather has arranged itself into sun, rain, or snow, and it
cannot be all at the same time (though just at the moment it
seems to be trying here where I live in West Wales). We can
explore as empirical fact the relationship between structures

and the processes of which they are part, and how different constellations are, or are not, related.

We use the term 'order' to describe a particular arrangement of some class of structures that could be otherwise: rocks can create a variety of landscape structures, air and water molecules can arrange themselves into different weather patterns. We use the term 'coordination' to describe the processes that sustain a particular order of structures, and the structure so produced. Just as we have a choice of timescale, we have a corresponding choice of structural scale: in neuroscience whole disciplines are based around choices of scale that differ by just an order of magnitude, and their respective experts find it quite hard to talk to each other.

Finally, and most important, we have a way to understand what happens when we start to discuss systems in terms of 'value'. The key is to see the discussion of value as primarily a shift in perspective and language in which we take the system in question – the particular scale and scope we have chosen as of interest – as a matter of concern; we look at the processes in terms of being 'for' that system and having consequences for its survival – looking over its shoulder and seeing the world from its point of view: what is it like to be a spoon on the string?

A point of view on the world: the value shift

> *We propose to define value as the extent to which a situation affects the viability of a self-sustaining and precarious process that generates an identity.*
> Ezequiel di Paolo[9]

EVERY living organism establishes a point of view on the world – it creates a web of significance. Let us suppose, for example, that a particular bird we are interested in requires a certain tree as part of its habitat for food and nesting. If

that species of tree is now attacked by an invading insect that
kills the tree then the bird may vanish from this ecosystem.
The bird is a dynamic identity, as we have discussed in
the previous section; it is only alive as part of a pattern of
relationship. From the point of view of the bird it finds
itself as a centre of some values such as 'habitat' and 'food'
in the surrounding ecosystem of which it is a part. Suppose
we also find that the insect is thriving because long term
climate cycles mean that the winter is no longer cold enough
to kill it off and so its numbers are expanding rapidly and
threaten the whole forest. Now the forest can be seen as a
system-in-question that also creates a perspective of value, in
which the insect is a predator. For an animal there are food,
predators, mates, habitats etc. For an ecosystem there are
planetary processes at play that impact it as a whole. When
we name a structural identity we simultaneously name a set
of relational processes that sustain it – the universe as seen
from the perspective of that identity. The language of value
is simply a move that we make to adopt the concerns of a
particular system and see its proximate pattern of relations,
and the wider universe of which it is a part, in terms of its
own 'interests'.

Every dynamic system identity is sustained as part
of a wider pattern of processes. There is no standard
terminology for describing the world as a set of many
interrelated processes played out through many dynamic
identities, though this is the main subject matter of the study
of complex adaptive systems. We can explore such systems
without needing the concept of 'value', though we may still
identify a system in question and investigate how it functions
as part of the whole and the nature of the relationships in
which it takes part. Equally, we can adopt the language of
'value' in our investigations and describe exactly the same
phenomena as revealing patterns of interlocking significance
for all the identities in play; then we can describe the whole
pattern as a 'value constellation'. A value constellation is the

same as an ecosystem, but described in terms of the values 'for' each living structure that comprises our level of interest.

Value is for a life, in a pattern of relationships.

Values are always in play

A living identity is always in motion, reforming itself and being reformed. Autonomy is always partial, and contingent, always at risk. A single organism actively moves around, eating, excreting, and maintaining its identity over the span of its life, and perhaps reproducing. That particular organism is part of bigger processes of life, seen in the species and ecosystem of which it is a part. We have described value as for a life, in a dynamic pattern of relationships. 'Value' names all the ways we might discover that relate a particular identity to the play of the universe as a whole.

For any thing that is concerned with its own identity there is an infinity of such values, because there is an infinity of possible paths it might take through the world, an infinity of processes to become part of, and each step reveals different opportunities. Now, if you are a lowly bacterium, with a short life span, that space of possibility may be quite small, and its contingent nature not much under your control. On the other hand, evolution may have equipped you with some useful tricks for extending your reach in space and time: some bacteria have ways of living over much greater life spans than higher organisms by suspending the metabolism and becoming inert for many years, awaiting the conditions for life to continue. As we move higher up the animal kingdom, lives become much richer in the types of value that connect an identity with its context; shelter, mates, competitors, packs, hunting grounds, and so on open up a wide field of choice for the contingent life.

At the moment we undertake the shift to the perspective of value for a life we find a paradox. If we take on the

interests of part of the system, then at the same moment
we find that the system as a whole has distinct 'values'. Life
on earth, seen as a system (evolution, or Gaia, if you will),
proceeds through individual lives, but without privileging
any particular one of them, or any species. Individuals and
species come and go while life goes on. Each life finds itself
in a value constellation that provides some conditions of life
and growth, and through its own life it carries forward the
flow of life for all the others. Yet like vortices in a stream, it
is the stream that continues, not any particular form of life.

That means that each life finds itself suspended within
ambiguous relationships that are essential to its growth but
that signal an unfinished, and unresolved, tension with the
origin of those relationships in the overarching process from
which they flow. This tension is found between experiencing
the values of being-for-itself, and being-as-part-of-the-
whole. The philosopher Jonas talked of finding ourselves
between the polarities of life: being and not-being, self and
the world, form and matter, freedom and necessity[10]. Our art
is constantly probing and exploring this experience and its
temporary resolution in patterns of life, love, hate, fulfilment
or despair. We are constantly finding the human and making
our own lives in the possibilities of the present.

Culture – the condition of being human

> *Without man, no culture, certainly; but equally, and more*
> *significantly, without culture, no men.*
> Clifford Geertz[11]

YOUR life goes with you, and you cannot leave it behind.
We will never know what book an author would have
written next, or what a friend would have said about a new
experience, but they leave behind something of themselves
in everything they did and the trace it left on our shared
culture. We can look at that life, and through anything that

we can share with it we can look for a deeper understanding of that life, our own life, and the relationship between them.

Species vary hugely in how much their behaviour is 'given' at birth, and how much they must learn in the course of each life. Learning vastly increases the adaptability of an individual and its community to the particular circumstances of their life – finding the best water hole, shelter, dangers to avoid, source of food etc. At the human level our species has taken the potential of learning further than any other, enabling us to construct, share, and pass on an immensely rich and resource-full collective culture. Personal growth into the shared culture, and participation in it, is the very condition of becoming human.

In this essay we are using 'culture' in the most inclusive sense, to capture the entire field of human activity prefigured in, and continuous with, the social processes we share with all other forms of life. Think about some very diverse fields of human activity, such as family life, farming, scientific research, the games of chess and football, religion, medicine, ballet, storytelling, and so on. Our culture is composed of an unlimited variety of such shared activities, with meaning passing amongst and between them all the time, each one sustained by its own pattern of shared intention.

I have found no generic term that can be used for these patterns, so I have appropriated the term 'genre' from its use to name artistic forms. To signal its wider meaning in these essays I will adopt the usage of 'cultural genres'. 'Culture', then, carries both the all-inclusive meaning of all the patterns of shared activity and expression (cultural genres) that make us human, and a narrower everyday use in which it is concerned with those sorts of shared meaning that lie at the humanistic end of the spectrum – the artistic genres that explore what it means to be human and to live a particular life. It is the all-inclusive meaning that we want to use here in order that we can see more clearly the distinctive role of artistic forms of expression and the role they play in other cultural genres.

We note here that although our culture is mediated to a very large extent through signs and symbols, we can create patterns of shared meaning between us without symbolic forms. Meaning is based in our embodied nature: we are cultural beings but we are first physical and vital beings – if we trip we fall, if we do not eat we starve, if we are not nurtured as babies we will never thrive. Our experience is mostly embodied, and embedded in our social lives, and our culture is carried forward in and through all forms of shared activity which tie one life to another, in something as simple as the rituals of a shared meal, for example. Human life is a qualitatively rich extension of the ways other creatures relate to the world, but rests on the same systemic principles and is continuous with them; our lives are lived within one set of ecological principles that extend 'downwards' to all life, and 'upwards' to the full richness of our artistic imaginations.

Unreasonable effectiveness

> *Music itself should not be used for political or any other purpose. But although you cannot make music through politics, perhaps you can give political thinking an example through music. As the great conductor Sergei Celibidache said, music does not become something, but something may become music.*
> Daniel Barenboim[12]

How do we make sense of a book, a map, an equation, a message, a game of football, a dance, and a life? We must relate the particular instance to the general field of shared meaning which our culture sustains amongst us.

Mathematics is one of our cultural genres. Pure mathematicians explore new branches of mathematics, motivated by the desire to discover new results for their own sake – maths for maths' sake. Part of what sustains

this is just the passion of those people who do it, but there
is also a broader cultural engagement because of what the
physicist Eugene Wigner famously called the 'unreasonable
effectiveness of mathematics in the natural sciences'.[13]
Mathematics advances in ways that are deeply entwined
with all our naturalistic sciences, supporting within them
the means of their expression. And so there is a constant to
and fro between maths and other disciplines, each enriching
the other (whether or not money is ever involved). These
sciences are also pursued both for themselves and because
they find themselves taken up into other cultural genres in
mutually informing patterns of knowledge and activity.

As with mathematics, so with art. Perhaps the first cave
painting was done out of sheer enjoyment of the expression
in itself – art for art's sake. Once done, it opened up a new
way for us to relate our selves one with another. Painting
has become a cultural genre, as has dancing, story-telling,
music and so on. Great art of any form has an unreasonable
effectiveness to relate us to each other in our experience
of the world. And so it intertwines with all our culture,
infusing it with the means to express what we find to be the
general experience of being human, and the particular path
of our own life. Just as an ecosystem has species, such as the
oak tree, that create a context of life for hundreds of other
species, so in our culture, artists – those for whom 'making' is
their vocation – create 'trees of meaning' around which many
species of individual meaning can flourish.

Bringing forth a world

> *Enaction: a history of structural coupling that brings forth
> a world.*
> Francisco Varela[14]

In the simple example of spoons swinging from a string we
saw how a pattern emerges from several elements coming
into a dynamic relationship which then changes what

each element is able to do. Adding more spoons changed the repertoire of possible behaviours each element could achieve, and if you could imagine being one of the spoons then your experience of the world would have changed – you would have discovered new potentials arising from your basic capabilities as a thing in the world.

Our cultural genres link up our lives, and in so doing change what it is possible for us each to do, to experience, to be. This is not metaphor, it is as real as a piece of string changing the behaviour of a spoon. Through our participation in cultural genres we change the path of our lives. Unlike the spoons, because we are living organisms, we are not bound moment-by-moment to just one sort of interaction. We can be connected in an infinite variety of ways, each one having a distinct significance, meaning, or value, for the path of our life.

Francisco Varela and his colleagues coined the term 'enaction' to describe this idea that the world we inhabit, and the embodied mind through which we experience it, arise together as a single pattern that is in constant motion. They called this process 'bringing forth a world'[15]. The essence of this approach to understanding our lives as beings in a world of significance is two propositions. First, that we play a role in defining reality, in the sense that any living being brings forth a world of experience conditioned by the needs of its own identity. This does not deny reality, but puts ourselves into an active role in bringing forth our experience of it[16]. Secondly, since our cultural systems are inherently social and historical, individual experience always arises in the extended interaction of the members of a community amongst themselves and with their wider context.

This enactive view lies at the heart of the ideas developed here. In the next essay we turn to a particular way of exploring the worlds that are brought forth in our shared lives by developing the concept of the *currency* of a cultural genre – just how we link ourselves up with varieties of cultural string.

3: ART IS THE CURRENCY OF EXPERIENCE

THIS essay puts forward three related ideas about the relationship of ecology, economy and experience that, while they draw extensively on related work, are each in some respect novel, and have not so far as I know been put forward in this way before.

First, we can bring the concepts of ecology and economy back into productive relationship by generalising the idea of economy beyond that of the system of exchange coordinated by money to a more general concept of *a coordinated pattern of human activity enabled by a currency*. In this way we will see that an ecosystem contains many economies each with its own currency, which support different ways for us to pattern our shared lives. This will allow us to put the discipline of economics where it belongs – inside ecology, and economies where they belong – inside ecosystems. Like the concepts in the previous essay, these ideas are quite general in scope, and go beyond the immediate concern with the role of art in our culture, but are a necessary foundation for that discussion.

Second, it has often been said that we are all artists. Here I want to take that thought into the centre of our experience of being human, by making the assertion that we are the artists of our own lives. This way of thinking will allow us to move in a principled way between the third person languages of ecology and economics that *describe* our lives, and the first person language of experience that concerns what it is like to *live* a life.

Finally, these two ideas are brought together to discuss how our first person experience is joined with our collective cultural journey by proposing that we understand *art as the currency of the economy of experience*.

Healthy economies

In the previous essay we found a way to talk about value – it describes the significance of something for lives that are lived in a dynamic pattern of relationships. There is not one universal 'value', as if it were an abstraction like energy; to talk about value is to explore how connecting living things together allows certain sorts of patterns of significance to arise. These patterns connect the value of something for an individual to its value for those around them – they bring forth a world of value in a particular cultural genre.

In this essay we will explore how in human society we extend these patterns of significance into what we can call economies which vastly enrich the patterns of valuation amongst us. There are two basic ideas here. First, is that the notions of an economy and its currency can be generalised so that money is just one special case. We shall broaden our idea of economy to include a more general class of cultural genres that share the property that they are coordinated through the use of a currency. We shall see that economies resolve the infinity of individual perspectives into a shared pattern of valuing.

Second, is that the valuing supported by an economy is continuous with the ecological pattern from which it arises – an economy is properly understood within an ecological context.

Having achieved this generalisation of the concept of an economy we will be able to explore art, money and other things in a common language, and begin to see what we might mean by talking about the health of the cultural patterns in which they are embedded.

We'll start with money. If you owned all the money in the world, but suddenly the rest of the world ceased to recognise the value of money, then yours would become useless. This would be a sudden and extreme case of the ordinary experience of inflation. In the case of money, which is used in relations between people to support trade and exchange, we immediately see that it only 'has' value because it is used in a pattern of relationships. The pattern of relationships that make money work well are those that lead to what we would then call a healthy economy. For example, high inflation generally causes all sorts of problems with the proper functioning of money and so modern economies have lots of tools to try and prevent it. You don't have to be an economist to grasp the idea that for money to be money, it has to represent exchange values in a reasonably consistent way as things are traded around, and we shall probably suffer some strange effects if it changes rapidly – if, for example, the money I spent in the morning for six apples, only signals the value of three apples in the afternoon. This would be considered a sign of a healthy *market* if it signalled a shortage of apples, but an unhealthy *economy* if it is the result of inflation.

   This simple example introduces several ideas that we will be able to use more generally to broaden the idea of a currency beyond money to other aspects of our culture including art. First is the idea that we connect the experience of value to a particular class of 'thing' – in this case money. Secondly, the value in this class of thing for an individual has to be sustained in a wider system of relationships and activities in which the thing has value for others. Thirdly, that there are some quite specific statements that can be made about how that wider system of relationships should be working to allow value to function in a way 'proper' to the topic of discussion. Finally, when the system is functioning properly, we can regard it as healthy, even though we might not always like specific outcomes – in fact it is a measure of health in the system that it can reveal and support certain sorts of conflict and competition. It is the very health of the economy that allows competition for scarce resources to be signalled by price, that will lead to changes in behaviour of buyers, sellers and producers: if that means I cannot afford the apples today, then so be it.

Before turning to the arts, we will look at a couple of other examples so as to get more used to this way of thinking in which we identify the particular class of 'thing' like money, and develop an intuitive notion of health for the system in which it works.

Scientific research proceeds by sharing the results of experiments – measurements – and a central part of this process is publication in peer-reviewed journals in which those measurements are carefully reported and related to the canon of knowledge in the appropriate discipline. If we place the measurements in the role of money, then we can make similar statements to those that we made above. A published paper and the results it contains has a particular relationship to the research it describes; it is not the research result, but represents it for the purpose of establishing relationships with other people. It has a value for the author that is only realised as the paper is taken up into the pattern of relationships of the scientific community to whom it is addressed. For that wider system to work as it should, there are many conventions and processes that must operate properly, regardless of the specific content of the paper: accurate reporting of results, fair and thorough reviewing, non-plagiarism, and so on. When the system is working properly it allows, in fact requires, vigorous debate and disagreement at the level of the content, until it is either rejected or admitted into the current body of accepted knowledge.

We can see that the system of money and the system of scientific publication have important similarities, and also that they are very distinct systems. We also know that when these two systems are connected we have to be very careful we do not disrupt the proper functioning of the central components. When the commercial logic of money, exchanging money for a desired outcome, is allowed to interfere with the proper role of a research paper – for instance by biasing the reporting of results to the hidden interests of a sponsor – then we see that the health of the research system has been damaged.

For our second example consider democratic government. Electoral systems lie at the heart of democracy, and their integrity is so important that mature democracies have very extensive systems dedicated to maintaining their health and ensuring their proper operation – votes must be handled as carefully as money. As before, it is a measure of the health of the underlying system that the democratic debate is itself rich and full of conflict. The dangers of money perverting the democratic system are well known. But we can also note that the democratic system is very different from that of scientific publication and that trying to connect these two systems also produces new problems for us to address. The role of evidence in the progress of science is not quite the same as the one it needs to have in the process of democratic debate on important social issues, and our societies are still feeling their way forward on how this connection should be brought about.

This last point illustrates that the very processes that promote system integrity must themselves keep changing to take account of changes in their context – monetary systems have to deal with innovations in financial instruments (and deal with expensive mistakes caused by bad ones, as we are now discovering); research must take account of the new intellectual commons created by the Web; etc.

We are accustomed in everyday language to mean by 'the economy' the cultural patterns created by the exchange of money. We also find writers discussing 'the attention economy' or 'the experience economy', which generally means exploring the role of experience, attention or whatever in the context of 'the (monetary) economy'. Here we want to do something different. We want to see money and the patterns it creates as just one instance of a general phenomenon in which something that we share – a currency – creates cultural patterns, which we will call economies.

This usage strengthens our language for the discussions in hand. Ecology is the discipline which studies ecosystems; an ecosystem is a specific instance of living organisms sharing a habitat, including humans. It is easy to slip into the usage of talking about the ecology of a particular species, or the ecology of culture, or whatever, but it is clearer if we reserve 'ecology' for the name of the discipline and talk about species within ecosystems, because the whole point of ecology is to study the overall systemic relationships among all the species that belong together. Within an ecosystem there are many different types of pattern that coordinate the lives of all the individual organisms; activity that is coordinated by a currency is just one sort of pattern that we find in human ecosystems.

To summarise, from now on we will take the position that all life goes forward within ecosystems, and that these ecosystems have many overlapping economies within them as part of their patterns of coordination. The discipline of economics is thus a subset of ecology. We now need to bring our understanding of the arts into the same language.

Shared horizons: the relativity shift

Relativity teaches us the truth of relationship, not the relativity of truth[17].

RELATIVITY is the key to an understanding of value that brings together individual and shared experience, subjective and objective points of view. We can explore this through the example of our experience of the horizon: only when you realise that your own horizon arises from where you stand can your mind properly grasp that you are standing on the globe of the earth. There is no doubt that each of us standing on the deck of a ship at sea experiences the horizon. This is a direct, personal experience. It is also true that for each of us the horizon is centred on ourselves, and therefore unique in the real objective sense of lying on a slightly different place on the earth; the closer we stand to each other the closer these horizons are on the globe, but they are, and must be, distinct. It is a condition of the experience that it is yours and mine. A rainbow is the same, it is centred on the individual as a condition of its existence as an experience. To an independent observer there is no 'one' horizon or rainbow that is the source of the individual experience, there is only the relationship between particular individuals and the earth as a whole. The objective existence of a horizon is contingent on the presence and point of view of a subject. As a matter of simple fact, there is no horizon to be found anywhere on earth until we introduce an observer.

There is an infinity of possible horizon experiences and they are only ever personal and particular; this is not a metaphor or a mystery, it follows from the mathematics of being in the world. Yet the experience of the horizon is something that we can name and share between ourselves as human observers, and as situated experiencers of the horizon. Experience is brought into cultural view by that act of shared naming or representation through a picture.

Some creatures have this experience (birds we assume), and others must lack it (those that lack sight); only humans have found ways to share it by naming and representing it, and in doing so it becomes not only yours and mine, but ours. In becoming ours, *experience is put into motion between us*.

The essence of relativistic thinking is that every subject creates a unique point of view, or frame of reference on the world, and that there is no background universal frame of reference. However, we can find ways of transforming between each point of view such that universals become visible to us. Science has found principles of relativity that relate to the most general categories of experience (space, time, mass) and makes systematic transformations between them. In this essay we are working towards extending such an understanding to art and culture; the foundational idea is to regard art as the transformation of personal horizons into the shared culture of humanity.

In art and culture we bring the duality of shared/individual experience into view: we give a common name to a unique experience; we explore just what it feels like for me to have that experience that is at once mine and universal – that can only come about because I encounter something that is not me in my own particular, personal way. As we encounter the experience of a horizon we discover something about ourselves – the nature of situated sight. And of course there are many dimensions to that experience: the setting sun, colour, wind, and so on. And each of these opens up another form of my being, a way that my being in this place and this time reveals something more about how the world and my experience relate to each other.

All living beings, humans included, find themselves as individuals filling a particular place in an unfolding history of other lives, some similar to their own and others vastly different. Each living being comes into a shared history of dynamic relationships, taking part in processes that sustain it and to which it contributes. Each being, by the nature of the fact of being a particular identity, occupies a unique path in space and time, and therefore has a unique experience of its place in the world, and contributes to the uniqueness of every other experience. This is as true of a bacterium as it is of a human.

Humans are exceptional in the richness of the cultural forms that we use to pattern our shared lives: mathematics and science, art and culture, money and markets, all set up different types of pattern of living experience. By structuring our shared experience they constitute ways for identities to live together, they bring forth different worlds that change the possibilities of the human, and that is their 'value'. Recall, that this is no metaphor – each cultural genre connects lives together and in so doing changes what each life can be for itself and as part of the whole.

We are the artists of our lives

Each mortal thing does one thing and the same:
Deals out that being indoors each one dwells;
Selves – goes itself; myself it speaks and spells,
Crying What I do is me: for that I came.
Gerard Manley Hopkins[18]

For this significant life, this certain significance of nature and
history which I am, does not limit my access to the world, but
on the contrary is my means of entering into communication
with it.
Maurice Merleau-Ponty[19]

LET's go a little deeper into the idea that every life defines
a distinct and particular form of value that is more or less
shared with others. This will reveal more of what is meant
by the relativity shift and help us find where the value is that
we are so concerned to build up. Whatever we might say
in abstractions and theories about life in general, life itself
is expressed through particular and individual lives that
have a beginning and an end. As a simple matter of fact,
whatever one life shares with another it also, by the nature
of the case, inhabits a unique situation of space, time and
circumstance in the history of the universe. The universe
has not had time to explore much of the possibilities of life.
And since every life is part of the situation of every other,
there are infinite possibilities which are to be resolved into
a particular life. If we want to understand the value 'of'
something in the context of a life, then there is no possibility
of a general answer; we must adopt the concerns entailed by
the existence of that particular identity where and when it
finds itself.

To keep on solid ground, revisit the examples of food and
horizons that have been discussed before. 'Food' is the name
of a category of relationship between living organisms and

their environment. When we adopt the concern that a living organism should continue to live, we see food as necessary to that process. Suppose, however, that in a famine a mother deprives herself of food for the sake of her family, or in a time of societal conflict someone goes on a fast as a means of protest. Do we then question the value of food and decide that it is merely subjective? Or, if we open up to understand the other motivations of life, do we rather gain a more precise insight into the relationship of food to other processes of identity? Might not a book or a play help us to explore and understand these different relationships by taking words like 'food', 'deprive', 'protest', and reconfiguring them? Did the mother consider herself as deprived of food, or giving of love; was this protest a gesture of defiance or solidarity, and defiance against whom, or solidarity with whom?

As we continue this enquiry, it as if we are trying to reveal the origin of the horizon: where do we have to place an individual such that these particular values together create the human experience that we are familiar with? Where is the cultural globe on which we can place all these words such that we can again feel that we are standing side by side and seeing the 'same' horizon? And since every life is unique, this quest is unending. All the language of food, love, protest, and every other term of our shared culture must be questioned, because this life with its particular concerns has given it a unique meaning.

Culture is both shared and personal. In so far as it is shared it has to be temporary and incomplete, because it configures our experience only through the lives that have gone before. It is as if we wake to the world with a description of the horizon that we must now make our own. There really is a horizon experience, but what it means for this life in the progress of its identity from life to death is something that only this life can find out, and in doing so, pass on a new understanding to those who will follow.

The value of art is precisely that it concerns itself with reflecting the experience of a particular life in its own terms, and bringing that into the infinite conversation of shared culture.

Many of us feel that we don't make any art in our lives. We enjoy our particular taste in music, may play an instrument, and have all our interests, but don't ever produce anything that we would consider to be artistic – that's for others to do. We enjoy experiencing what others have done, and share that experience in our social life, but the making is not for us. Yet, as we have seen, the making of culture is inherently a shared endeavour of everyone who participates in it. Every life reveals something unique because it gives a unique form to the process of living a life. Whether or not I ever give up food for my family, or choose to go on hunger strike, my life will cast a meaning on the concepts of food, love and protest; they are part of the cultural conversation. That significance grows with my engagement in the choices that have gone before and that are transmitted to me through the culture in which I find myself.

I must find the human for myself, and I pass on my discoveries, for good or ill. We can look out from a mountain top and be inspired by the wonder of nature or see lands to be conquered; we can listen to Beethoven quartets and find comfort and renewal in distress, or terribly, as we now know, go to work to exterminate people in the morning. How could somebody have seen that view, had that experience, and made that choice? Each of us has to search for our own answer, by questioning for ourselves what it is we are seeing, where we are standing, and how our own identity and the choices it reveals will contribute to the next stage of the conversation. If that is the horizon that I thought we shared, where is the other person standing? How can I place their experience and mine such that we are both standing on a shared earth? How deeply must I enquire into the particular path of that life so that I can connect to it through the shared experience I thought we had? Now that I know that, how does my own life reveal choices that I did not know I was making, and that will now echo down the generations? I must plainly bring many more dimensions into play than I had before when I naively thought we all saw things in the same way.

It is in this sense – that we live our lives as part of the infinite conversation of culture – that I want to say that *we are all artists of our own lives*. This is a statement about art, culture, and all our lives. It makes of culture the shared repository of human experience; it sees that repository as always an unfinished work that is constantly remade by everyone's life; and it sees art as concerned with the central task of enquiring into the human at every place and time, and connecting the general cultural inheritance with the unique and particular experience through which it is continued and renewed.

It seems to me that this is what Ursula Le Guin meant when she wrote that 'art makes truth, but does not tell it'[20]. Art directly puts into play the shared experience in a way that enables me to re-examine what is true – it is a making that permits specific meaning to be made; it enables a new personal and shared telling of truth that must be accomplished by engaging with it and bringing particular experience up against it. As Peter Brook put it, 'Meaning never belongs to the past; it can be checked in each person's own present experience' (Brook 1996).

Art is the currency of experience

> *To understand the "idea" in a work of art is therefore more like having a new experience than like entertaining a new proposition.*
> Susanne K. Langer[21]

Reading is a passionate act. If you read a story not just with your head, but also with your body and feelings and soul, the way you dance or listen to music, then it becomes your story. And it can mean infinitely more than any message. It can offer beauty. It can take you through pain. It can signify freedom. And it can mean something different every time you reread it.
Ursula Le Guin[22]

ANYTHING can be money: shells, stones, marks on a pot, pieces of metal with the queen's head stamped on them. Anything can be art: pictures, dances, ideas, found artifacts, performances, lives. What makes anything money is that we agree it should be so. Money records commitments. For it to work everyone must agree on what it is – at least enough that we can use it. Of course £1 is worth different things to different people, but it buys the same. Likewise, for a word to be a word, it must circulate among us doing roughly the same job for everyone, though its usefulness will vary on each occasion. And a piece of art becomes art when it passes amongst us as the currency of our experience.

What does it mean to have an experience? Experience is the condition of our life at any moment while we are alive. As living beings we have at any moment a vast range of possibility – I'll avoid the word freedom for now. You are sitting in the airport waiting for your flight: will you look out of the window, read the newspaper, do the crossword, send a text, watch the TV screen, go and have a coffee, shut your eyes and dream of your next holiday, meditate, chat to the person next to you... each variety of experience connects us to something that plays a role in configuring that experience. It may be 'inside' us, as a memory or a thought, or 'outside' as a thing or person.

Some of the things that configure our experience are just there, whatever we think about them – the sun will rise whatever I think. But others are only there because we, and others we share our life with, have ways of agreeing they should be – the dance can only continue because we all know the steps. Such things are reflexive experiences, they reflect back our engagement with them into our experience of them. As I sat in the airport thinking, perhaps a picture or a tune came into my mind. It seemed to bring with it something of the essence of the dance, just what it felt like to have that rhythm shaping and holding my movements.

Have you ever been stuck, wanting to leave a message for someone, but not having any pen or paper? Out on a walk you have not met your friends where you expected, and you want to go off and find something to eat. How will you signal to them that you were there, and where you have gone? At moments like this you realise just how hard it is to bring a random collection of objects into a shared relationship of meaning with other people. The first problem is just making it clear that what I am leaving is a message at all. I need to ensure that something I do is responded to in a particular way. Then my friends must relate this message to our shared culture of words, maps, and intentions and find some way to make sense of it – it must have some internal consistency that they can bring alongside this particular moment to reveal its meaning.

To see something as art is to respond to it as an expression of personal experience, as the trace of a life. To become art, something must move from being private to circulating amongst us as a means of sharing the experience of being human, taking its place in the continuous dance of our culture. In doing so, like a dance, its meaning is made, shared, and reflexively remakes our experience of our selves.

Art is the currency of experience.

Economies

> *Beauty is Nature's coin, must not be hoarded,*
> *But must be current, and the good thereof*
> *Consists in mutual and partaken bliss.*

John Milton, Comus

LET's summarise the main points and see how we can bring this set of ideas back towards our day-to-day concerns.

When things enter into a dynamic relationship then qualitatively different behaviours emerge – spoons discover a rhythmic potential, humans find the power of language. It is a mistake to attribute the new quality of the overall system to any part of it – it belongs simultaneously to all the parts and the whole. If we regard the presence of this quality as an important measure of health or wealth for the individual parts or the whole then we must be concerned with all the parties to the relationship. This is the essence of ecological thinking – that we identify qualities of a system of dynamic relationships and understand their mutual dependence. Health and wealth are just two modes of discussion concerned with the presence or absence of processes and structures within these relationships: understanding what critical degrees of participation are required to maintain a minority language within a larger community, for example.

There is an inexhaustible potential in all the different ways that people, places, and things in the world might be configured, and at every moment each choice sends the world down a slightly different path; to continue our example, as individuals choose which language to use in a multilingual environment they change the future course of each language and its potential to be a vehicle of shared experience for themselves and others.

We can use the general concept of *currency* to characterise one of the ways in which human society creates patterns of relationship that connect us while promoting individual diversity and choice. The role of a currency is to bring individual choices and judgements together into a widely shared pattern of activity and experience. We have defined such a pattern as an economy.

Money is just one currency of human life, and the money economy is a pattern of exchange of things and services. It is the distinctive quality of the money economy that it promotes the movement of things from being part of one set of relationships to being part of another. This is the very purpose of money and the foundation of property rights – the right to take something and do what I like with it. Technically this is known as 'alienation' rights, and the term conveys the essence of the function of money, which is to move something from a pattern of relationships to some other, alien, pattern[23]. This is how money works; within the economy of money, it allows things to be exchanged in ever more complex patterns of trading.

There are things that can be exchanged, things that we think shouldn't be, and things that simply cannot be: I have to live my life, and you have to live yours. I can share my taste in music, but I cannot give it to you, sell it to you, or take yours by an act of violence. You might give up your life for me, but you cannot give me your life. These are inalienable properties. When we speak of them as 'properties' we are using a meaning of the word as a noun of quality, meaning something that is one's own, or special.

It makes sense to talk about the concepts of health and wealth with respect to a particular economy, in terms of the processes and structures within it that allow it to function and preserve its distinctive qualities. Something is a currency because we treat it so, with a respect for its health. We have a sense of what it means to maintain the integrity of money, research, democratic voting, and language, as currencies that support distinct patterns of activity.

Each economy is a unique pattern of shared valuing

WE need to develop further the relationship between the ideas of economy and value. As a first step we'll take a simple example: the way competitive sports work as an ongoing shared pattern of activity. This example is chosen because sport is very different from art, is bound up with money, just as the art world is, and clearly is enjoyed not for its instrumental value but for itself. People don't (I presume) go to a football match because of the monetary value of football or for its instrumental outcomes in their lives – football has monetary value because people are passionate about it and go to the matches; it has some sort of 'intrinsic' meaning-in-itself in their lives.

In the nature of sporting competition the end result is a ranking of performance – there are winners and losers. This comes about through scoring or judging: either the activity itself defines an unambiguous result by shots won, goals, timings, position crossing a line, etc, or there have to be judges who take a binding view of the quality of the overall performance and award points and positions after the fact. Either way, there is a description of the outcome that is agreed by all. For the purpose of this

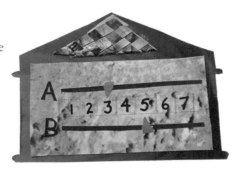

discussion we will refer to the outcome as a 'score', whether it is points or positions. By considering this score as a 'currency' we draw attention to three ways it operates.

First, the score reduces everything that happened in the game itself to a description or label: the score does not describe the action except in the very roughest sense that a 5-0 score at football for instance will tell you something about the relative quality of the teams that day. Secondly, for the score to be recognised as valid we treat it the same way we treat other descriptions, which is that other people would score it the same. Even when we have judges, and recognise that different judges might reach slightly different results, we hope that there is a degree of consistency that everyone can agree with, or the whole process falls into disrepute. Finally, it is the use of the score in a sustained and consistent way in an ongoing series of games that allows individual events to be built up into a tournament, league, club ladder and so on. These three properties are what we need for our wider discussion so we will take each of them in turn.

Look first at the way that the score is both about the game, but is much less than the game. Imagine all the commentaries during and after the game as it is discussed in the media and by the fans: was it a good result, a good game, who messed up, and so on; for those with an interest in the game and the players there is no end to the possibilities of discussion. Each of these discussions relates one game to another, exploring different understandings of what makes up the essence of the game and our enjoyment of it. The score is just one, very particular way, of relating games to each other, but for competitive sports it is a particularly important one that configures all the other meanings. It is that primacy of keeping account of winning and losing that constitutes something as a competitive game; there are plenty of other ways to play together that don't involve winners and losers. It is the scoring that constitutes the game *as* a competition and not something else. Of all the ways we can make sense of the game, one is given a distinguished role in coordinating our collective experience of individual events into the sport as a whole.

Secondly, we can see the importance of the score being understood in a shared way if it is to achieve its intended purpose of linking up our collective experience of the games. If we choose to play a 'friendly' match in a competitive sport then we might not even bother to keep score, but the moment we want to connect events together to take their place in a sequence of games, the consistency of scoring really matters. We then devise ways to ensure that we all reach an agreement on the score, with judges, umpires, equipment, appeal panels, and so on all dedicated to resolving ambiguities into an accepted result. We all have to agree what it is that the score is 'about' and how everyone involved can reach a shared assessment of the game in the score, even though we might disagree vigorously about more or less everything else.

Finally, the understanding of how to score the sport develops as we use it over more and more games. Not only do we reach a shared resolution of one game into a score, but as a sport is played we reflect the scoring back into the rules of the game to further refine the competition, so that it comes to represent more and more clearly what we regard as the real essence of that particular sport. We seek to make it represent the heart of the competition in the fairest sense. Over time, what we 'sense' in our experience of the game in terms of the relative performance of the players, we 'make sense of' in the score that records its outcome. Of course, this collision between the sensed experience of the game and the sense conferred by the score is then the subject of endless debate and banter amongst the rival spectators as to whether it really represented who was the better team or player, but that is all part of the fun; to agree would be boring.

Thus we see how our collective use of scoring puts a 'value' on each game, by determining the worth of the game in the ongoing competitions of which it is a part, and our collective understanding of what makes a 'good' game in this particular sport. The score is the currency of the competitive value for that particular sport and its 'economy'.

We can now make some statements that should seem very obvious within this example, and will carry forward into our wider discussion.

Value, understood as scoring, is particular to every sport; there is simply no meaning at all in attempting to score one sport by the scoring system of another – this is referred to as two different measures being 'incommensurable'.

The value described in the score is related to, but different from, the experience of the game itself. Imagine taking your child to a game and telling them just to watch the scoreboard to follow the game – they would miss completely what was going on and afterwards would lack the experience of it. If we want to talk about the game and the experience of it then we will have to put it in terms different from the score[24]. To discuss the experience of the game is to discuss its 'intrinsic' values within the economy of the sport.

If we acknowledge that one score only has a little to say about the particular game to which it refers, then the accumulated scores of many games have even less to say about why we would care to keep playing the game and teaching it to our children, and are in no useful sense a store or signal of value that the sport might create in our lives. Again, there is no surprise here; scoring is used to compare games, not to describe them. The wider discussion of why play that sport is just a broader discussion of both its intrinsic value and its relationship to the rest of our lives.

We cannot hope to make scoring a way of discussing these other values of the game by any means at all; while we can deepen the scoring to represent finer grain aspects of the game, if we ask people to assign scores to all the other ways they value the sport in their lives, or even worse, expect them to use scores to compare different games, then ever more meaningless conversations will result.

The difficulty of using the score to discuss these other aspects of the game is not because the score is somehow an 'objective' measure and the other aspects are hidden in some 'subjective' realm of private experience; the difficulty is that the score is the result of a practice of collective judgement – a measurement, or valuation – that is intended to put aside all the other aspects of the game. The judgement of scoring is no more or less subjective than any other way of talking about the game – we might say the shared judgement of the score is made by our 'collective subjective'.

The score, functioning as the currency in the economy of the sport, can be said to establish the 'economic value' in that economy, since that is what we all agree upon, and everything else that actually *was* the game can be said to represent its 'intrinsic value'. People will disagree, and enjoy disagreeing, about the intrinsic value, not because it is somehow mysterious, wholly subjective, and immune to systematic enquiry, but precisely because it can be discussed and the discussion is inherently open-ended – there is no end to the interpretations that can be made of what went on, and the existence of the score merely gives the discussions a particular edge.

To recognise that there are many score-values that are strictly incommensurable – that is, useless for making comparative valuations – is not to say that we cannot discuss the experience of games individually or in comparisons of relative worth, but to say that we must seek some other means to do so – some other currency of shared valuation.

With this understanding in mind we can return to the more complex economies that we are interested in of money, art, and life in general. For each case the same basic idea is stated in three ways that are intended to be equivalent, to help establish the language I am aiming at:

The score is the currency of a competitive game that becomes a shared sport.
Scoring is the currency of the economy of a sport.
The economy of scoring coordinates individual games of a particular kind into a collective competitive sport.

 Votes are the currency of democracy.
Votes are the currency of the economy of democracy.
The economy of democracy coordinates individual preferences into collective policies and powers.

 Measurement is the currency of science.
Measurement is the currency of the economy of science.
The economy of science coordinates individual phenomena into collective 'objective' knowledge (constitution of the world into scientifically discussable objects within a shared canon of knowledge by means of measurement).

 Money is the currency of exchange.
Money is the currency of the economy of exchange.
The economy of exchange coordinates individual use values of alienable property into collective markets.

 Art is the currency of experience.
Art is the currency of the economy of experience.
The economy of experience coordinates individual lives into the collective experience of being human (constitution of persons within a shared field of life).

To bring something into circulation in an economy is to measure it according to the shared denomination of value in the currency of that economy. The old vase in the attic that we valued for its place in the home is put into the antique market and finds a monetary value. Or we put it into the local museum where it is valued for its place in local domestic history, or into the art gallery because it turns out it is a fine example of a particular period of ceramics.

Each economy creates a sort of shared valuing amongst diverse individual activities. Keep hold of our trusty piece of string here to help us remember that each spoon was able to swing on its own, but by linking to others this behaviour has altered into a qualitatively new one.

Similarly, we can trade things, make decisions, study the natural world, and have personal experience without the aid of any economy, but an economy opens up a wider field of possibility for that linkage than would otherwise be possible. In doing so, it widens and deepens the quality of that sort of value for the life in its ongoing pattern of relationships. So, we could barter and exchange things without money, but money vastly extends the possibilities of markets because money releases each act of exchange from having to involve goods moving in both directions.

The currency of art supports us in valuing each moment of our life with respect to our understanding of the human – the human as others have experienced it, put in relation to the particular choices in front of me here and now.

4 : ECONOMIES OF LIFE

I must say... to my economist colleagues: Consider the economy as forever becoming, burgeoning with new ways of making a living, new ways of creating value and advantages of trade, while old ways go extinct. This too is the proper subject for your study, not just allocation of scarce resources and achievement of market-clearing prices. The economy, like the biosphere, is about persistent creativity in ways of making a living.

Stuart Kauffman[25]

THE previous essay put forward the idea that we should generalise the concepts of currency and economy beyond their conventional use with reference to 'the economy' (singular) that is the pattern of our lives coordinated by the currency of money. In this essay I want to start exploring how we can think about multiple economies – what keeps them both individually and collectively healthy, and how different economies should connect. In particular, I want to contrast the roles of the economies of money and art.

There is an important warning before we start. Many people will feel uneasy about importing the language of economy ever deeper into our lives. I share that worry, but it is economics that must be reformed to come into line with a broader understanding of life. Traditional economics as taught in the mainstream curriculum was formed at an unfortunate time. It is dominated by ideas of physical equilibrium that bear no relation to the dynamic processes of life which is always maintaining itself far from equilibrium – for a living organism equilibrium is death. Many problems, theoretical, practical and of far reaching consequence have arisen from economics going up that path. For the last couple of decades the leading edge of economics research has been concerned with bringing economics back into contact with the understanding of living processes by which order arises in complex systems, bringing ecological thinking into economics; it is with this breaking edge of research that I am concerned[26]. That also means that while I believe these ideas are well supported by the latest thinking, there is much here that is tentative and will no doubt need better formulation in the future.

My goal is that we should connect thinking about the arts to the vanguard of economics research and free it from the constraints of a narrow interpretation of value dominated by traditional thinking on money and markets.

Being economical

> **economic**: *relating to private income and expenditure...in a wider sense: the administration of the concerns and resources of any community or establishment with a view to orderly conduct and productiveness.*
>
> Oxford English Dictionary

THERE are two everyday uses of the term 'economy' that we need to distinguish. At a small scale when we talk about personal and domestic economy we are thinking about the particular choices concerning resources made by an individual or household to fulfill its own purposes. At a large scale, when we talk about the economy of a country we mean both the allocation of resources by the whole community and also the way individual activities combine into what the OED calls the 'orderly conduct' of our collective economic affairs.

At the small scale, traditional economic thinking tends to locate 'value' in the resources that are passed around and 'consumed' by a particular participant in an economy. More recent thinking on economic value challenges this[27]. Take the example of going to the shops and buying some tomatoes.

At the moment when you leave the shop you have given up some money and you are carrying a heavy weight. Only when you get home and do something with them – cook a meal for your family or friends – do you get the value you wanted. In this sense, we understand that we always co-produce the value of things within our personal economy. This is just as true of enjoying a work of art. As we read the poem, or contemplate the sculpture, we must produce the experience by combining our own resources with the potential of the work before us. Value is realised, as we have seen throughout these essays, through the pattern that comes into being at that moment. I might have put the tomatoes into a bowl and painted a still life.

Income and expenditure is not just about what passes in and out of my personal economy, it is about the choice of which pattern of life I engage with, which economy I choose to join at each moment. Thus, at the large scale, the value that is circulating in each economy depends in the end on what each participant brings to it from their own living potential to join and continue the pattern: the pattern of buying and selling, of voting as a citizen, of listening and telling stories.

It is an odd notion that we measure the national economy by GDP – the market value of goods and services each year – not by what is actually achieved by shifting all that stuff around. That's because it is very hard to measure what really matters – the value each person did or did not manage to create in their personal economy with the forgotten book on the shelf or the treasured antique. Money is not value; money coordinates patterns of exchange within which value can be realised in lives that use the things exchanged.

Splitting and sharing

I am working with two groups of associated ideas and trying to describe a particular relation between them. We have, on the one hand, imagination, synthetic thought, gift exchange, use value, and gift increase, all of which are linked by a common element of eros, or relationship, bonding, 'shaping into one.' And we have, on the other hand, analytic or dialectical thought, self-reflection, logic, market exchange, exchange, exchange value, and interest on loans, all of which share a touch of logos, of differentiating into parts.

Lewis Hyde[28]

CONSIDER the examples given earlier of different economies (science, sport, democracy, art, money): each one operates on a different combination of factors that are alienable – that pass from one participant to another – and factors that are inalienable because they belong to the pattern itself. A research paper, for instance, is something that is passed around, copied, stored, protected with rights, sold, and generally treated as an exchangeable thing, but it 'works' by coordinating the understanding of the world amongst those who read it – an understanding that is neither wholly of the individuals nor of the community, but is a quality of thought in motion amongst them. This understanding simply cannot be alienated from the individuals who hold it – it can only be shared amongst them and others who choose to participate in the same economy of knowledge.

There are many forms of currency (of which measurements in scientific papers are an example) that primarily promote patterns of sharing rather than patterns of exchange. Hyde discusses these as examples of what he refers to as 'gift economies'. Thus, this essay can only acquire value by circulating in a pattern of conversation through the currency of language, drawing on the meaning each word has for you in our partially shared linguistic history. It can only 'work' to the extent that it brings our minds together to construct a shared meaning, which relies on the health and wealth of our common word hoard. I cannot send you my understanding packaged up in words; I can only hope that the words, like string between us, will bring out a quality of mutual understanding that does not yet exist.

It would be easy to slip from assuming that the cooperation in a shared pattern of which I am speaking here necessarily implies agreement of purpose, intent, outlook or anything else. That may be true, as in cases such as open source software, wikis, and other cultural endeavours which have a common purpose as their defining quality. But more generally, as was discussed in the third essay, economies promote diversity, and it is a measure of their health that they generate a dramatic expansion of diverse ways to participate in a pattern. For example, it is the extent to which we can express ourselves clearly that we can disagree most vigorously. It is important to keep in mind the notion of 'coordination', that was introduced in the second essay, which describes our participation in a pattern without assuming alignment of purpose: think of grass, rabbits and foxes and their shared patterning of life in an ecosystem.

How economies connect

How do the different economies of our lives interact? Recall the example in the first essay: if we take a tree from the wood to make a piece of furniture, we perturb the systems of health in the forest. Take too many and the forest may collapse and die. This is not just about movement into the money economy – the same happens in reverse, as the music industry is finding; if recordings of music are appropriated for free from the money economy of music by illegal file-sharing then the whole production system starts to collapse while the parallel pattern of file-sharing thrives. We can now generalise the way we described this problem. Rather than being a tension between ecology and economy, it is a tension amongst economies within an ecosystem.

Each economy contains elements that are alienable, that are passing around between the participants, but it also has overall inalienable patterns of identity and relationship that make it what it is. If you connect the alienable factors to some other economy and they are taken up into a different pattern of circulation, there is a risk that you may damage or even destroy the first economy. This is not just about money. There was an issue recently where the BBC was criticised for failing to give air time to a charity fund-raising programme. At stake was the distinction between reporting and promoting, and the BBC's insistence on maintaining a clear distinction between the two that they felt was in danger of being blurred. I don't want to comment on the rights or wrongs of that case, but to make the point that rights and wrongs were being discussed because, according to this analysis, there was a practical issue: which economy should their air time function within – charitable promotion or news reporting.

Economies are always connecting through the lives that are generating them, and these living agents must make constant choices of how to relate their own life to the conditions they find around them – how to configure resources into patterns that continue their own activity as part of the whole. In so doing they are constrained by maintaining their own integrity and the collective integrity of the shared pattern.

Integrity of economies

WE do connect economies, but it matters just how we do it. For example, in democracies we use our votes to decide policies on the use of money – in a sense, we 'buy' money with our votes. But we are very clear that we should not use money to buy votes because this corrupts democracy; it corrupts the currency of the democratic economy. Similarly, we use money to support research, and have a spectrum of societal arrangements from commercially funded work at one end to publicly funded at the other. We expect very different conditions to apply in each case. The relationship between research, funding, and democracy becomes even more complicated. As we add more economies we are faced with a bewildering and constantly shifting set of possibilities which we must configure so that the economies are mutually supportive rather than mutually destructive.

Each economy can only thrive because we get its boundaries right and allow it to operate according to its own internal logic while meaning and money pass to and fro across the boundaries with other economies. Our human society is forever finding new ways to relate economies to each other that keep them all 'healthy', that is, each operating in ways that preserve its integrity while supporting each other.

Each economy must preserve the integrity of its own activities so that they can be done on their own terms, and thus in a way for their own sake. For some reason artistic genres are particularly attacked if they pursue art for art's sake but this is as ridiculous as criticising a jockey for racing for racing's sake or a physicist on the new Large Hadron Collider particle accelerator for doing physics for physics' sake. The confusion is now easy to understand: within the race, the jockey must indeed operate according to the values that connect all the participants and make the race a race – anything else is to defeat the whole object. And surely physicists who do anything other than good physics will not find what they are looking for – you certainly can't persuade new particles such as the Higgs boson to turn up for any political imperative to improve society or any monetary incentive. The race and the experiment are each part of a particular cultural economy in which the individual event must sustain, and be sustained by, the integrity of the currency which relates it to other events. If you link part of that activity to another by connecting it with a different currency you will distort it because it will take part in a different pattern. This applies to any pair of economies – it is just as wrong to bias a race outcome for some political favour as to do so for money.

Health and wealth

EXPERIENCE has shown that planned economies tend over time to be self-defeating. The very point of an economy is to promote a certain sort of unity in the diversity of individual activity. If the individual choices are taken by a single authority then we prevent the operation of the processes that cause the economy to function: trying to make choices for people means that we remove a source of information from the system and reduce its diversity and adaptive potential. This is as true of language as of money: over time dictionaries have to follow the use of language, not attempt to dictate it.

On the other hand, when economies are elevated into supreme arbiters of value they also damage the whole ecosystem of which they are only a part. There is no one economy to which we can delegate the well-being of our lives. This is just a simple consequence of the fact that any economy is a pattern that is less than the whole of nature – there are other patterns outside it (some of them are economies) that function as part of the health of the whole. Again, we are just reminding ourselves of the ecological perspective – the whole does not exist for the sake of any one part, and a part does not control the whole; an economy is just a part, like a particular food web in a forest. We might do art for art's sake, or physics for physics' sake, but we can rely on neither of them to sustain our individual and collective well-being over time. Each is just one way to pattern our shared life.

It is now clear that discussions of health and wealth of a particular economy involve taking that economy as a 'system in question' and making the value shift to explore its unique perspective on the whole ecosystem of which it is a part. As we explored before, that shift will reveal the tension between being-for-itself and being-as-part-of-the-whole.

Meaning and money

THE economy of art is concerned with sharing our experience of being human and renewing our means of shared expression. A work of art is the product of a life, reflecting the uniqueness of that life. It is a thing made, and shared as a work of art. It allows us to transform the irreplaceable, un-transferable perspective we each have into a shared quality of life. It brings forth new qualities through relating one life to another, and in doing so, creates new potentials and rhythms of life amongst us. It enables us to coin new human meaning, or refresh old understandings in the perpetually changing situations of life.

There is thus a distinctive role for the economy of art in the shared pattern of our lives. It is to coordinate amongst us our exploration of all the economies of life from which we choose the pattern in which to take the next step on our own path. An artistic response to our human world brings all our fields of meaning into play: it dissolves and dissipates our world in order to recombine and reorder it[29]; it allows us to step away from reality in order to re-engage with it afresh, bringing forth new fields of significance; it temporarily removes the lived significance of our means of expression from practical consequences so that they can become even more consequential. It enables us to re-interpret and discover new ways to live our own integrity – to find the human in the unique and particular circumstance of our own life.

All through this discussion I have avoided discussion of 'values' in the way that we use that term in everyday language when we talk about 'our values' – meaning principles by which we guide our individual and collective lives. The connection that now appears between the way value has been developed here – as a perspective on the whole created by a living identity – and this sense of principle is traced through the notion of integrity of an economy. Questions of principle, of what to value how, arise as we decide which economy should take precedence at any moment – into which pattern something should be taken up, knowing that in taking part in a pattern it loses some qualities and acquires others. These questions matter so much precisely because so much is at stake – something that is taken out of a system changes it, perhaps in profound ways. It can be even more troubling if something is functioning according to the 'wrong' economy. If players take a bribe to throw a game then they have damaged the integrity of the game. It was the integrity of their news service, not the merits of the charitable cause, that was at issue in the BBC case.

The arts, seen in their most general role as putting stories of the human into motion amongst us, support our continuous re-evaluation of the integrity of the patterns of our lives. They help reveal how identity is arising in each economy of which we are a part, and therefore give us more freedom to *produce* our own life in relationship to others: bringing all the possibilities of life into the particular integrity of our own. As artists we envision the pattern that we aspire to make; as producers we bring together the resources from which we weave our part of the whole. Money helps us all move resources around in service of the production of our shared lives; it cannot build the shared stories by which we live.

CAN we use ecological thinking to understand how the arts work in society? That question was the starting point of our investigations in the International Futures Forum. In this final essay we offer some directions for using the concepts we have developed for policy and management in the arts and what is called the 'cultural' sector (in the more limited sense of culture that is the common usage). We have built these ideas through a number of conversations, and in particular with Watershed[30] in Bristol. A companion document[31] gives the full case study. These are very preliminary applications of the ideas and in no sense represent an overall set of policy prescriptions, but we have found these initial attempts fruitful.

So, our answer to the question is: yes, ecological thinking can open up fresh and useful ways to think about how we organise our affairs to allow the arts and culture sector to thrive, and can help us tackle the long standing debates about value in new ways. The main goal here is to give a flavour of the direction these investigations are taking, to stimulate interest in the ideas, and invite more people to join the exploration.

Art and 'the arts'

> *For many people 'art' is part of the fabric of their lives, while 'the arts' are something institutional, and separate from their day-to-day experience of the world.*
> Catherine Bunting[32]

I cannot in this paper attempt to survey the history of 'the arts', something of which in any case I know almost nothing, and indeed one reviewer has pointed out that any attempt to pin down the meaning of this term as I have done here is already an 'inflammatory act'. However, again and again in the conversations that shaped this essay people would make the point that is summarised in the quotation above, that in our culture 'the arts' (or Arts, with a capital A) are often disconnected from the pattern of our everyday lives, and that we must find ways of discussing them that restore the connection. That is what I am trying to do.

What has caused this fault line? One way to look at the disconnection of 'the arts' flows quite directly from the analysis here, which is to see the way that a 'work' of art functions both as currency in the economy of experience, and as tradable commodity in the economy of money. Indeed, the rise of our notion of Art has a lot to do with tradability and the fact that artworks can be displayed as indicators of wealth and prestige[33]. It is precisely the alienability of Art as product that connects the economy of experience to the economy of money. Indeed, one explanation of the value of art describes it as primarily concerned with a display of sexual and general evolutionary fitness – the more flamboyant the display, the more you are showing you have resources to spare and must therefore be a good choice of mate. Given that money is the main indicator of general resource (because it gives access to all forms of alienable resources), the economy of art is bound up with all the ways in which money supports power and prestige in our societies. The point here is not that there is anything 'wrong' with this relationship of the arts and the signalling of status, but rather it is just one resolution of the relationship between the economy of art and the other economies of our lives. We want to give a much wider sense of that relationship than the one that is limited by the ways art can function *within* the economy of money.

In recent times discussions have broadened to include the notion of 'the economy of experience'. But those that I have found are in fact discussing the role of experience goods in the economy of money, and so are still dominated by the notion of money as 'the economy'. The central point of this whole set of essays is that we should instead see our lives as a pattern of multiple economies whose interaction we are constantly negotiating. Each economy configures a particular shared pattern of human life and has its own particular measures of health and wealth and must be understood in its own terms. Our concern must be to understand how to link these economies together so that they all grow in appropriate and mutually supportive ways, and to tackle this we need a way to view the long-term rise and fall of different patterns of value creation. We have found two tools useful in tackling this in practical situations: three horizons and dilemma thinking.

Three Horizons

The mathematician and philosopher Alfred North Whitehead talked about a 'creative advance into novelty' as the ultimate ground of all being. Generating richer and more intense conversations, opening up new possibilities, triggering new connections, new configurations – this is what it means to generate 'more' meaning, advancing into novelty. We have found the 'Three Horizons' model of longer term change a useful framework for understanding the dynamics of this advance[34].

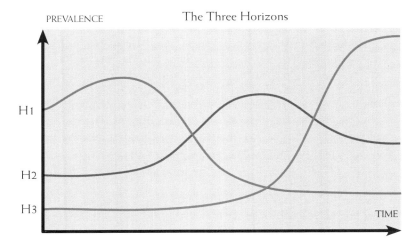

Fig 2: The three horizons represent shifting patterns over time as conditions change

The first horizon – H1 – is the dominant system at present. It represents 'business as usual'. As the world changes, so aspects of business as usual begin to feel out of place or no longer fit for purpose. In the end 'business as usual' is superseded by new ways of doing things.

Innovation has started already in light of the apparent short-comings of the first horizon system. This forms a second horizon – H2. At some point the innovations become more effective than the original system. This is a point of disruption. Clayton Christensen called it the 'innovator's dilemma': should you protect your mature business that is on the wane or invest in the innovation that looks as if it might replace it?

Meanwhile, there are other innovations happening already that today look way off beam. This is fringe activity. It feels like it is a long way from H1, based on fundamentally different premises. These are the first stirrings of a third horizon – H3. This horizon is the long-term successor to business as usual, the product of radical innovation that introduces a completely new way of doing things. We always have the chance to configure new sources of abundant life.

The advance into novelty is an adaptive transformational process, a journey towards the third horizon. It is by no means an easy process. For the first horizon's commitment is to survival. The dominant system can maintain its dominance even in a changing world either by crushing second and third horizon innovation, or by co-opting it to support the old system. These behaviours lead to variants on the smooth transition depicted above – notably the common 'capture and extension' scenario in which innovations in H2 are 'mainstreamed' in order to prolong the life of the existing system against the grain of a changing world.

The meaning—money dilemma

THE central idea of dilemma thinking is to take conflicting requirements and use them to frame a space in which you search for a creative resolution[35]. The key insight of this approach is that resolving such dilemmas is always a process of creative insight achieved in the moment; it is never stable, can never be reduced to rules, and must always be lived – like keeping a sailing boat upright while sailing as fast as you can in a stiff wind. In the terms we have explored in these essays, dilemma resolution between meaning (the purpose of our lives at any moment) and money (access to resources) is an act of artistic production. A healthy creative ecosystem is one in which they are constantly re-configured so as to feed and replenish each other, the sweet spot combining money and meaning.

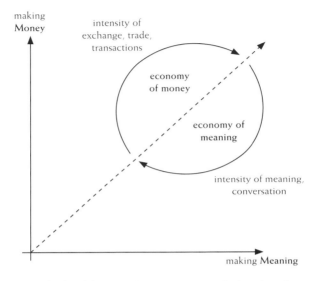

Fig 3: The healthy creative ecosystem – balancing the economies of money and meaning

Cultural innovation

It is this second shift [wide availability of personal computing linked through the pervasive networking of the internet] that allows for an increasing role for nonmarket production in the information and cultural production sector, organised in a radically more decentralised pattern than was true of this sector in the twentieth century. The first shift [to an economy centred on information] means that these new patterns of production – nonmarket and radically decentralised – will emerge, if permitted, at the core, rather than the periphery of the most advanced economies. It promises to enable social production and exchange to play a much larger role, alongside property- and market-based production, than they ever have in modern democracies.

Yochai Benkler[36]

THREE Horizons and dilemma thinking provide ways of thinking about cultural innovation – how a culture advances over time. A healthy culture, a creative ecosystem, will always be generating new ideas, new possibilities, new meanings. Today's highly connected world, as Benkler describes in *The Wealth of Networks*, has effectively released a Cambrian explosion of information and possibility. There is an unprecedented abundance of chaotic human cultural potential.

But to become meaningful – in our terms, to take its place in the economy of meaning – this chaotic potential needs to be configured into cultural patterns and relationships, 'genres', that release its capacity for shared meaning making.

The isolated, novel, visionary acts of artistic invention in horizon three provide a growing edge for the established first horizon culture. As they are configured in the second horizon these isolated instances of creative vision are brought into relationship, creating new patterns of shared meaning, new cultural genres. And these new genres in turn become recognised as an important part of our culture, settling into an established role within an expanded first horizon. This is the process of cultural innovation. The way that the Web has spawned a whole collection of new models of collaborative production in almost every field of endeavour is an example. Or more specifically to the media sector, the way computer games are evolving beyond their initial audience into use in a wide variety of settings such as education is a good example. This process of transition is never smooth since it involves vigorous debate over which values should predominate in the new patterns. The economy of art promotes the health of these debates.

To be a cultural innovator, therefore, is to operate in the second horizon space, configuring the chaotic abundance of meaning in the third horizon. The claim is that artistic innovation has a particular role to play in opening up new forms of collective patterning of our lives. Recalling the quotation from Sergei Celibidache in the second essay where we considered the 'unreasonable effectiveness' of art: *music does not become something, but something may become music.*

We make the move from invention to innovation in the economy of meaning when 'something becomes music'. That process is at the heart of a healthy creative ecosystem.

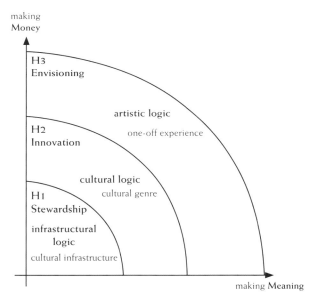

Fig 4: In the cultural innovation system each of the horizons has a different logic, moving from one-off experience through new cultural patterns, or genres, to finally bedding down in the cultural infrastructure

The Producer

THE critical competencies in the second horizon innovation system are those of the producer. This is a role whose importance is increasingly recognised in the arts. Many impressive cultural productions today are not the product only of cultural organisations or individual artists, they are enabled by an individual with the skills and energy required to orchestrate the creative process and to bring an artistic idea to reality.

The producer's role is fundamentally to sit between the first and third horizons, brokering the relationship. The producer must appreciate both the financial logic of H1 and the artistic logic of H3 in order to bring a project conceived in the visionary imagination to fruition with the backing of funders in the money economy.

Kate Tyndall's book *The Producers*[37] illuminates the role beautifully in a series of interviews. Here is Helen Cole for example: 'I have always liked ideas at the early stages, at that point of uncertainty, when the balance between what is possible and what is not is constantly being redrawn... works have emerged from this indefinable alchemy... some kind of chemistry takes hold. As producer, it is my job to recognise this moment, to spot the possibilities, to listen to the dreaming, to replay the thinking, until the work takes shape and becomes real'. Or, more succinctly, Helen Marriage: 'the role of the producer is to take responsibility'. This is not the same as project management. The producer is invested personally in the process as a participant. There is an emotional engagement. The process carries with it the visionary and inspirational quality of its H3 origins. The producer is inspired, has belief, and will pursue a project in ways that H1 might not understand. The producer cares, beyond reason.

The producer is operating according to what we might call a 'cultural logic'. It is about fashioning potentially valuable, emergent H1 order out of the chaotic abundance of the meaning economy in H3. The producer is a market maker in the economy of meaning, a true 'cultural entrepreneur'.

This is a hugely valuable set of skills in today's world. The digital age has resulted in an abundance of opportunity for mixing and remixing, participation, collaboration and co-production. The skills to orchestrate and configure this abundance, especially utilising the potential of the new digital technologies themselves, are not only valuable in cultural organisations. Every organisation now needs to learn how to master the cultural logic that lies behind successful cultural entrepreneuring. For in time, like reading and writing, this logic will become a necessary part of our cultural infrastructure – one that we need to master in order to live and thrive in a meaningful world.

Navigating the meaning—money dilemma: the Watershed example

If we now turn to Watershed as an example, we will see that it is a complex human ecosystem which is the setting for many overlapping patterns of value, many economies.

Watershed in Bristol is a venue that has become a central space in the city for cultural exchange, promoting engagement, enjoyment, diversity and participation not only in film but in more diverse media arts and the city's burgeoning creative economy. It is a place that overlaps multiple channels of physical and online experience in film and related media – one of a number of cross-art-form and media venues in the UK that have flourished in the age of clicks as well as bricks, as described by Tom Fleming in his report *Crossing Boundaries*[38]. It is a space that people and organisations naturally gravitate towards to stimulate creativity and to 'make something happen':

Watershed is a prime example of a highly connected, flexible, porous piece of cultural and creative infrastructure, of which there are too few examples. Watershed is more than just an arts cinema. It is at once a cultural centre, a business broker, a social networker, a research and innovation facility, a café/bar, and a cultural tourist attraction.

UK Creative Economy Programme

The cinema brings film and, more broadly, the digital moving image into the economy of meaning as a currency of experience. At the same time, like all of us, Watershed operates in the economy of exchange. The economy of exchange coordinates individual perceptions of use values into collective markets. This is the familiar economy where the currency is money.

As a system, Watershed can operate to maximise its returns in either money economics or meaning economics. If it concentrates only on meaning it may produce exceptionally valuable work but go broke – the artist in the garret. If it concentrates only on money it may become highly profitable but will no longer offer participants the opportunity to enrich their understanding of the meaning of their own lives and what it is to be human. Money works best when it has no meaning – circulating in the system in order to enable exchange.

Watershed can thus be seen as operating in the dilemma space between these two economies. Through our conversations four approaches to this dilemma resolution emerged:

Keep a dynamic balance of money and meaning:

Watershed's innovation space operates in H2 – it gives a frisson of novelty to H1 and provides a focusing space for the abundance of possibility in H3. We can consider this in terms of the money—meaning field. Successful innovation will come in H2 from always seeking the balance point between money and meaning. This is about optimisation on both axes, not maximisation. In other words, aim for the top right corner (Fig 3).

Part of Watershed's value lies in the breadth and diversity of its networks, and its attractiveness as a partner which keeps those networks constantly refreshed. As a consequence it is always possible for Watershed to 'curate' appropriate connections, hook people into productive, apparently serendipitous, conversations. This is how imaginative play and possibility on the meaning axis is brought into communities, conversations and overlapping genres which help to shift the conversation towards the money economy whilst maximising the creative content.

An example of movement in the other direction is the Watershed café/bar. Many would see this as the part of the operation designed to generate maximum income and perhaps to subsidise some of the less commercial activities. But here too, consistent with maintaining Watershed's critical role as an H2 cultural innovation system, Watershed considers the café/bar as a central facility for creating meaning. It is designed to encourage conversation and chance meetings. People feel at home there and able to reconfigure the space to their own needs. It is where an important part of the value of Watershed's core offering is delivered in the conversations after the film that share the experience between viewers. It would be possible to degrade this environment by exploiting only its commercial potential. Some money is foregone in order to maximise the café/bar's contribution to the economy of meaning.

Move money to the margins:

Recall that the function of money in a system is to fragment and separate, to allow elements to be removed from one context and placed in another. It is a unit of exchange. And yet it is the overlapping of multiple economies in a complex constellation of value that is the essence of a creative ecosystem. Remember that where value is being created we nevertheless always have a choice about where to take out revenue, where to locate the interface with the money economy. In other words, we have a choice about which transaction to pay for.

Take, for example, the experience of going to the Watershed cinema for a film or an artist showcase. People come to see the event, perhaps because they trust the judgement of the programme selector, and knowing that they will be able to enjoy a pleasant drink in the bar afterwards discussing what they have seen with friends and strangers. Watershed carefully curates this whole experience, from the selection of the event to the cultivation of an audience to the welcoming nature of the bar space.

There are many options for taking out value in monetary terms. Watershed could charge for the cinema ticket, or a monthly membership, or rely on the food and drink charge at the bar, or charge a rent for time spent at a table, or charge by the number of words exchanged in the ensuing conversation. These last two are clearly absurd: because they bring the monetary transaction right to the centre of the experience, which changes it beyond recognition. We certainly need money to flow through the system, but not in a way that degrades the other currencies of value. Just as we pay to watch the football game but not to bribe the referee, so we need to keep the monetary transactions at Watershed at the margins.

Grow more producers:

One of the critical limiting factors at Watershed is the availability of the skills and competencies required for the role of producer. In order to build on its success Watershed needs to grow more producers. Fortunately, the creative ecosystem that lies at its core is the perfect breeding ground; what it takes to become a producer is experience. Not project management experience, but the special kind of experience described in Kate Tyndall's book: operating explicitly in H2 and providing 'the bridge between the work and the world' as Michael Morris puts it, or between the funders in H1 and the visionaries in H3. The producer needs a complex, messy, creative, diverse, highly-connected, H2 space in the money—meaning field in which to grow and develop.

Watershed specialises in this kind of environment and so has become a very effective *producer of producers*. This is rare and very valuable, in diverse fields way beyond the boundaries of the arts and cultural sector. It is easy to train project managers, but a rare gift to be able to grow producers.

Encourage participation:

The way to gain direct benefit from Watershed's innovation system is to participate in it. If you want to grow you need to plant yourself in the ecosystem. Like the producer, in order to innovate in this space and to benefit from the rich diversity of value and connections, you have to place yourself in the mix, participate in the process.

So those organisations already asking Watershed for advice with their own issues are encouraged to send an individual or a team to Watershed to work on them in the setting of the H2 cultural innovation system. They will generate new ideas and initiatives that will be appropriate for their own setting. And they will gain an experience of cultural logic in action that will be a valuable asset in their home organisation[39].

It is not only other cultural organisations that should be encouraged to participate. Cultural innovation, creativity and cultural logic are attributes that all organisations will need to master – especially those dealing with complex issues in overlapping economies.

Policy transition

DRAWING on the conceptual thinking in these essays, and
on our early experience in practice at Watershed, we can
start to discern the main outlines of a broader process of arts
and cultural policy transition. We suggest that the central
principle for developing a new approach is to build on the
concept of distinct economies that must be managed in their
own terms. In particular, this can be framed as managing
the dilemma between economies of money and meaning.
This essay is just the start of the exploration of how we can
achieve this, and we offer here a first draft of some guiding
principles about relating economies to one another so that
they, and the ecosystem of which they are part, all remain
healthy and wealthy in mutually supportive ways.

No economy must dominate

1. The ecosystem of our lives, as a system, is more than
   the economies that form part of it.
2. There are many overlapping economies; each has its
   own patterns of health and wealth.
3. No one economy can embody values that sustain the
   whole.

Maintain the integrity of each system

1. Each system has its own conditions of integrity.
2. Don't debase its currency.
3. Keep money at the margins.

Principles of sustainable exchange between economies

1. No economy can be sustained if it becomes solely a
   resource for another.
2. Observe boundaries and create loops of mutual support
   and integrity.

Manage the dilemma between money and meaning

1. Money coordinates patterns of exchange.
2. Art coordinates patterns of meaning.
3. Resolving the dilemma is a constant process of creative production.

Practise three horizon thinking within and between all economies

1. Create distinct policy mechanisms for stewardship of the first horizon and nurturing innovation in the second, while scanning for acts of creative imagination in the third.

One striking observation that follows from these principles is that arts funding is still very much based on funding individual organisations. As we have described, this makes a lot of sense in H1 where the primary task is consolidation and stewardship. But in H2, the domain of innovation where creative and practical ideas are born, the approach needs to be different. The direction of the policy transition we need to make is clear.

If we look at the way industrial policy has changed over the past 25 years we can see a shift from picking winners towards maintaining the enabling conditions for successful innovation: healthy markets, liquidity of money providing available funds for investment, business incubators to nurture start-ups, fluid relationships with research centres and universities etc. And we are gradually also making the more profound shift from seeing the environment as a limitless resource to something that needs to be sustained and renewed.

By analogy, cultural policy now needs to start making the same transition. But it will take time for the policy landscape fully to accommodate this discovery.

Innovation funding in the arts and cultural domain is still about picking winners; it needs to shift towards providing enabling conditions i.e. a healthy creative ecosystem, liquidity of meaning providing a rich source for new relationships, and a sustainable relationship between the commercial economy and culture as an abundant resource, between money and meaning. We also need to invent the equivalents of 'business incubators' and their surrounding infrastructure. We suggest that these might be thought of as 'regularly funded habitats', rather than as the typical first horizon Regularly Funded Organisations.

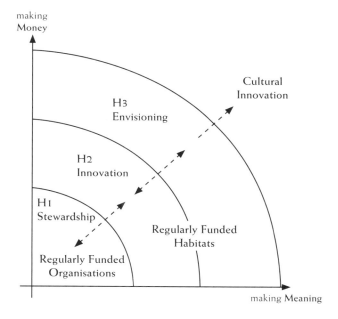

Fig 5: Horizon 1 has regularly funded organisations, Horizons 2 and 3 need regularly funded habitats for envisioning and innovation in the economy of meaning

There is a lot more work to do to turn the ideas here into working policy and management tools – but it is work that needs to be done, work that IFF will continue to pursue, and for which we hope these ideas have provided a useful start.

THIS set of essays is offered in the spirit of the gift economy; it will enter the economy of meaning if you give it currency, and I will be pleased if it becomes part of a conversation on the value of the arts in our lives and how they, and we, can best thrive.

ACKNOWLEDGEMENTS

MANY people have contributed to the evolution of these
ideas. My IFF colleague Graham Leicester has played
a central role all the way through the work. He had the
original insight that suggested this project might be put
together, and has acted throughout as the 'producer' by
assembling the resources that supported the creative work
and connecting it to other organisations and conversations.
He has also been a constant support in capturing discussions,
commenting on drafts, and putting in substantial effort
editing this final document – it would not have happened
without him. The early stages of the work were supported
by Mission, Models, Money[40] who took the risk to try out
this approach and enabled us to have some very stimulating
workshops with a wide range of people from the arts world.
I am also indebted to Dick Penny and Clare Reddington of
the Watershed who played a key role in bringing these ideas
into contact with real issues through an extended set of
workshops; we would not have got anywhere without them
and their creative engagement. There are not many people
who have the time and inclination to explore ideas of this
sort in an open-ended way and I am particularly grateful to
Judith Aston, Max Boisot, Clare Cooper, Fred Cummins,
Roanne Dodds, Jon Dovey, Ian Page, Rebecca Hodgson,
Tony Hodgson, and Rafael Ramirez who have discussed ideas
or reviewed drafts.

In presenting this work I was faced with a dilemma.
When you listen to a piece of music it is full of references
to other works, and yet you must make all those links for
yourself. When you read an academic paper you expect
the links to be made, and careful recognition of sources
is essential. The academic style of writing makes for hard
reading, and also implies that one needs to know the
sources to assess the material. However, while I have drawn
extensively on many sources and tried to invent as little as

85

possible, I hope to engage people with the power of this way of thinking entirely on its merits, just as a work of art must first engage us with the experience if we are to be motivated to find out more about it. So I have opted to write this in the style of an essay or opinion piece, absorbing the language of others into my own from sources which I identify in the notes, rather than constructing it out of carefully referenced points. If, as a result, I have inadvertently omitted to acknowledge a source, or appear to plagiarise, then I offer my apologies and will be pleased to make good such mistakes in a future edition.

REFERENCES

Barenboim, D. (2006). In the Beginning was Sound, The Reith Lectures, UK: BBC.

Beinhocker, E. D. (2006). *The Origin of Wealth: Evolution, Complexity, and the Radical Remaking of Economics*, Harvard Business School Press.

Benkler, Y. (2006). *The Wealth of Networks*, Yale University Press.

Blake, W. and G. Keynes (1966). *The complete writings of William Blake: with variant readings*, Oxford UP.

Boyle, J. (2003). 'Foreword: The opposite of property.' *Law and Contemporary Problems* **66**: 1.

Brook, P. (1996). *The Empty Space. 1968*.

Bunting, C. (2007). 'The arts debate: Stage one finding and next steps', Arts Council England: 11.

Coleridge, S. T. (1971). *Biographia literaria, 1817*, Scolar Press.

Curry, A., A. Hodgson, et al. (2008). 'Seeing in Multiple Horizons: Connecting Futures to Strategy.' *Journal of Futures Studies* **13**(1): 1-20.

Di Paolo, E. A., M. Rohde, *et al*. (2007). 'Horizons for the enactive mind: Values, social interaction and play.' Cognitive Science Research Paper, University of Sussex CSRP 587.

Fleming, T. (2008). Crossing Boundaries: The Role of Cross-Art-Form and Media Venues in the Age of 'Clicks' not 'Bricks', Arts Council England *et al*.

Geertz, C. (1973). *The Interpretation of Cultures: Selected Essays*, Basic Books.

Hampden-Turner, C. (1990). *Charting the corporate mind: graphic solutions to business conflicts*, Free Pr.

Hyde, L. (2007). *The Gift: How the Creative Spirit Transforms the World*, Canongate.

Ingold, T. (1990). 'An Anthropologist Looks at Biology.'
   Man (London) **25**(2): 208-229.

Jonas, H. (2001). *The Phenomenon of Life: Toward a
   Philosophical Biology*, Northwestern University Press.

Kauffman, S. A. (2002). *Investigations*, Oxford University
   Press, USA.

Langer, S. K. K. (1957). *Philosophy in a new key; a study in the
   symbolism of reason, rite, and art*. Cambridge, Harvard
   University Press.

Latour, B. (2005). *Reassembling the social: An introduction to
   actor-network-theory*, Oxford University Press, USA.

Le Guin, U. K. 'Author Talk, September 2006.' Retrieved
   8/9/2009, from http://www.teenreads.com/authors/
   au-leguin-ursula.asp.

Le Guin, U. K. 'A Message about Messages.' Retrieved
   14/10/2005, from www.cbcbooks.org/cbcmagazine/
   meet/leguin_ursula_k.html.

Leicester, G., Sharpe, B (2010). 'Producing the Future:
   Understanding Watershed's Role in Ecosystems of
   Cultural Innovation', Watershed.

Lewis, T., F. Amini, et al. (2000). *A general theory of love*,
   Random House.

Marsalis, W. and G. Ward (2009). *Moving to Higher Ground:
   How Jazz Can Change Your Life*, Random House Inc.

Merleau-Ponty, M. (1962). *Phenomenology of Perception*.
   London, Routledge & Kegan Paul.

Ramirez, R. (1999). 'Value co-production: intellectual origins
   and implications for practice and research.' *Strategic
   Management Journal* **20**(1): 49-65.

Sherrington, C. S. (1941). *Man on His Nature by Sir Charles
   Sherrington, OM The Gifford Lectures, Edinburgh,
   1937-8*, The University Press.

Tarde, G. (1999). 'Monadologie el societe (Oeuvres de Gabriel Tarde vol. 1).' *Paris: Institut Synthelabo*.

Thompson, E. (2007). *Mind in Life: Biology, Phenomenology, and the Sciences of Mind*, Harvard University Press.

Tyndall, K. (2007). *The Producers, alchemists of the impossible*, Arts Council England and The Jerwood Charitable Foundation, London.

Varela, F. J., Thompson, E., et al. (1993). *The embodied mind: cognitive science and human experience*, MIT Press Cambridge, MA [US].

Vernon, D. and D. Furlong (2007). 'Philosophical foundations of AI.' *Lecture Notes in Computer Science* **4850**: 53.

Wigner, E. (1960). 'The unreasonable effectiveness of mathematics in the natural sciences.' *Communications in Pure and Applied Mathematics* **13**(1): 1-14.

NOTES

1   www.internationalfuturesforum.org. The history of this project is on the site at www.internationalfuturesforum.com/projects. php?id=24.

2   (Leicester 2010) 'Producing the Future: Understanding Watershed's Role in Ecosystems of Cultural Innovation' by Graham Leicester & Bill Sharpe, is available from Watershed: watershed.co.uk/reports

3   "Wanderer, there is no path, paths are made by walking." Machado.

4   (Sherrington 1941)

5   (Marsalis and Ward 2009)

6   (Ingold 1990)

7   (Lewis, Amini et al. 2000)

8   (Blake and Keynes 1966)

9   (Di Paolo, Rohde et al.) This paper establishes the relationship between the enactive approach to cognition and the conception of value as I develop it here, and I owe a great deal to the paper for the way it articulates the concept of a web of significance cast over the world by a living organism.

10   (Jonas 2001)

11   (Geertz 1973)

12   (Barenboim 2006)

13   (Wigner 1960)

14   The enactive approach to cognition is the underlying philosophical approach that informs the whole of this essay. The seminal work is (Varela, Thompson et al. 1993) and an extended recent treatment of the philosophy is in (Thompson)

15   (Varela, Thompson et al. 1993)

16   (Vernon and Furlong 2007)

17   This is my own free rendering of a quotation from Deleuze – "Relativism is not the relativity of truth but the truth of relation" that is given in Latour (Latour 2005) p95 in the context of the relationship between relativism (anything goes) and relativity. Lacking the context of that discussion this version says what I intend.

18   'As Kingfishers catch fire, dragonflies draw flame'. Gerard Manley Hopkins.

19   (Merleau-Ponty 1962)

20   I have not been able to trace the original essay source for this quote, but have found it more recently still available in an interview (Le Guin).

21   (Langer 1957)

22   (Le Guin)

23   There is a very useful discussion of property rights and their relationship to the public realm, especially the concepts of intellectual commons in "The Opposite of Property" (Boyle 2003).

24   I am grateful to Fred Cummins for suggesting this example. Personal communication.

25   (Kauffman 2002)

26   (Kauffman 2002; Beinhocker 2006)

27   (Ramirez 1999)

28   This quotation comes from *The Gift*, by Lewis Hyde (Hyde 2007), which has influenced much of the thinking in this paper on the role of art, and in particular has helped me see the essential difference between the splitting effect of money and the synthetic role of art.

29   This is an intended echo of the passage by Coleridge on the imagination: "It dissolves, diffuses, dissipates, in order to re-create; or where this process is rendered impossible, yet still, at all events, it struggles to idealize and to unify." (Coleridge 1971)

30   www.watershed.co.uk

31   (Leicester 2010)

32   (Bunting 2007)

33   Max Boisot, personal communication.

34   (Curry, Hodgson et al. 2008)

35   (Hampden-Turner 1990)

36   (Benkler 2006)

37   (Tyndall)

38   (Fleming 2008)

39   For examples see two Watershed initiatives www.dshed.net, and www.pmstudio.co.uk.

40   www.missionmodelsmoney.org.uk

Publishers

TRIARCHY Press is an independent publishing house that
looks at how organisations work and how to make them work
better – both internally and in relation to each other and
their environment. We present challenging perspectives on
organisations in short and pithy, but rigorously argued, books.

The name 'Triarchy' comes from our founder Gerard
Fairtlough's theory that challenges the hegemony of hierarchy
in organisations and puts forward two alternative ways of
organising power and responsibility in order to get things
done: heterarchy and responsible autonomy. Our publications
offer a number of different but related approaches to
organisational issues from the fields of systems thinking,
innovation, cultural theory, complexity and leadership studies.

Our key partnership with IFF continues the practices of
breaking with established norms and finding new responses
to our surroundings: practices that are becoming increasingly
important as our natural, economic and social systems become
more volatile and unpredictable. These challenges require us
to embrace the potential of change rather than retreat towards
familiarity and stagnation, opening the door to intelligent
and innovative preparation for the future. IFF's thinking and
writing take significant steps towards this. This is our fourth
IFF publication, following *Ten Things to Do in a Conceptual
Emergency* by Graham Leicester and Maureen O'Hara, *Beyond
Survival* by Graham Leicester and *Transformative Innovation
in Education* by Graham Leicester, Keir Bloomer and Denis
Stewart.

Please tell us what you think about the ideas in this book.
Join the discussion at:

www.triarchypress.com/telluswhatyouthink

www.triarchypress.com
info@triarchypress.com

International Futures Forum

INTERNATIONAL Futures Forum (IFF) is a non-profit organisation established to support a transformative response to complex and confounding challenges and to restore the capacity for effective action in today's powerful times.

At the heart of IFF is a deeply informed inter-disciplinary and international network of individuals from a range of backgrounds covering a wide range of diverse perspectives, countries and disciplines. The group meets as a learning community as often as possible, including in plenary session. And it seeks to apply its learning in practice.

IFF takes on complex, messy, seemingly intractable issues – notably in the arenas of health, learning, governance and enterprise – where paradox, ambiguity and complexity characterise the landscape, where rapid change means yesterday's solution no longer works, where long term needs require a long term logic and where only genuine innovation has any chance of success.

Author

BILL Sharpe is an independent researcher in science, technology and society. He was a research director at Hewlett Packard Laboratories where he led research into everyday applications of technology and introduced scenario methods to HP to support long-range research and innovation. Since leaving HP he has specialised in science, technology and policy studies for business strategy and public policy foresight.

WITH a background in psychology he is particularly interested in drawing on leading edge research in cognition and systems thinking to find new ways of tackling complex problems. He is a member of International Futures Forum.

Illustrator

JENNIFER Williams is a critically acclaimed maker of hand made books, cut outs, photographs, illustrations, prints and puppets.

She is a trustee and member of the International Futures Forum and for 31 years directed the Centre for Creative Communities.